GODS AND GODDESSES IN
GREEK MYTHOLOGY

Michelle M. Houle

Enslow Publishers, Inc.

40 Industrial Road	PO Box 38
Box 398	Aldershot
Berkeley Heights, NJ 07922	Hants GU12 6BP
USA	UK

http://www.enslow.com

Library of Congress Cataloging-in-Publication Data

Houle, Michelle M.
    Gods and Goddesses in Greek Mythology / Michelle M. Houle.
        p. cm. — (Mythology)
    Includes bibliographical references and index.
    Summary: Discusses various Greek myths, including creation stories and
tales of principal gods and goddesses.
    ISBN 0-7660-1408-8
    1. Mythology, Greek—Juvenile literature. [1. Mythology, Greek.] I. Title.
II. Mythology (Berkeley Heights, N.J.)
    BL782 .H68 2000
    398.2'0938'01—dc21   00-028782

Printed in the United States of America

10 9 8 7 6 5 4 3 2 1

To Our Readers:
All Internet Addresses in this book were active and appropriate when we
went to press. Any comments or suggestions can be sent by e-mail to
Comments@enslow.com or to the address on the back cover.

Cover and illustrations by William Sauts Bock

▣ CONTENTS ▣

MAJOR GREEK GOI

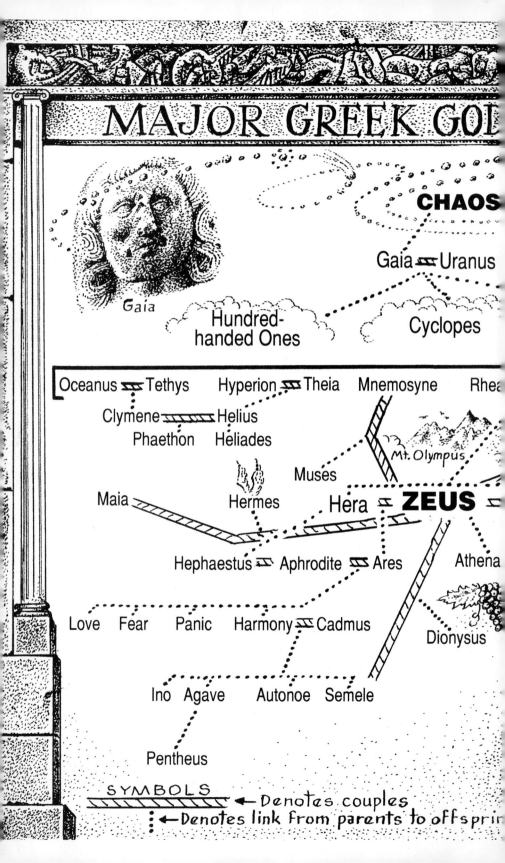

CHAOS

Gaia ⚏ Uranus

Gaia

Hundred-handed Ones

Cyclopes

Oceanus ⚏ Tethys   Hyperion ⚏ Theia   Mnemosyne   Rhe

Clymene ⚏ Helius

Phaethon   Heliades

Mt. Olympus

Muses

Maia ⚏

Hermes

Hera ⚏ **ZEUS** ⚏

Hephaestus ⚏ Aphrodite ⚏ Ares

Athena

Love   Fear   Panic   Harmony ⚏ Cadmus

Dionysus

Ino   Agave   Autonoe   Semele

Pentheus

SYMBOLS   ⚏ ← Denotes couples
⋮ ←Denotes link from parents to offsprin

AND GODDESSES

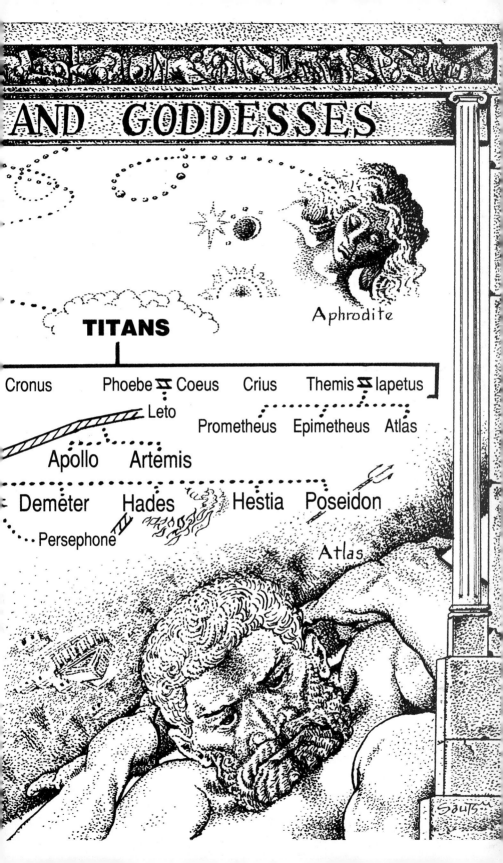

Aphrodite

TITANS

Cronus Phoebe ⚥ Coeus Crius Themis ⚥ Iapetus

Leto Prometheus Epimetheus Atlas

Apollo Artemis

Demeter Hades Hestia Poseidon

Persephone

Atlas

PREFACE

The word *myth* comes from the Greek word *mythos*, which means "story" or "speech."[1] *Myth* is often the word used to describe a story that explains events or objects that occur in nature, such as the creation of certain flowers or animals, the location of deserts or oceans, and even the origin and cycle of the seasons. Myths may also be stories about the origins of customs or traditions.

While some real events or characters may be represented in myths, these stories should not be read as if they are history. Though there may be elements of fact intertwined in their telling, these stories happen in a time and place that does not really exist, regardless of how real the setting may seem.

The Greek Landscape

The landscape of Greece has always played a great role in the development of its people and its myths. The country of Greece is located on the European continent to the east of Italy in the Mediterranean Sea. It is a country surrounded by many islands—some very small and some quite large, like the island of Crete. The Peloponnesus is a peninsula in the southern part of Greece. It is connected to the mainland by a thin strip of land, an isthmus, that is watched over by the old hill city of Corinth. The Peloponnesus is home to the important cities of Sparta and Olympia. Athens, on the other hand, is on the southern tip of the mainland in a region known as Attica.

There are many hills and mountains rolling across the Greek countryside. Therefore, while it might be snowy and cold in one part of the country, it can also be hot and dry in another. On the whole, however, the weather in Greece is warm, with sunny skies and relatively mild winters. The soil is dry and rocky due to the intense sun and rolling hills, and farming has always been difficult. Grains, such as wheat and barley, and fruits, such as olives and grapes, have been common crops throughout history. However, because it was difficult to tease crops out of this rough soil, the people who live in this area have also always depended, at least in part, on the sea.

Thousands of years ago, the Greeks were already great seafarers, and they sailed all over the Mediterranean. Because of their travels, the Greeks came into contact with people of many different backgrounds. They met and traded goods with people in Asia Minor and Africa, Europe and the Middle East. Every time the sailors came into contact with people from different backgrounds, they listened to the foreigners' stories and added them to their own collection. The extensive travel of early Greek culture helps to explain why there are many different versions of each myth, and why the myths of many different cultures often seem very similar.

History

People lived in the area now known as Greece for thousands of years, but very little is known about the area's earliest inhabitants. Archaeology, or the study of ancient civilizations, has taught scholars a little bit about the people who lived there between 6000 and 3000 B.C. Scholars believe that the early Greeks relied on farming and lived in small village-like communities.[2]

The years 3000 to 1600 B.C. are often considered the beginning of Greek culture and Western civilization in general. Scholars do not know much about the daily lives

Italy

Macedonia

GREECE

Mount
Olympus

Ionian Sea

Delphi

Ithaca

PELOPONNESUS
Olympia   Corinth
Mycenae
Sparta

Mediter

E·

Black Sea

Caucasus Mts.

ASIA MINOR

○ Troy

Persia

egean Sea·

Phrygia

hebes

C A

○·Eleusis

○·ATHENS

N

W · ○ · E

S

ea·of·Crete·

CRETE

anean·Sea·

Ethiopia (in Africa)

and customs of the people who lived on the mainland of Greece during this period. Like their predecessors, they seem to have been farmers. A lot of information, however, exists about the civilization then thriving on the island of Crete, where the legendary King Minos was thought to have lived. Beginning in about 2200 B.C., the people of Crete, called the Minoans, built fabulous palaces and ruled the seas with a strong hand.

In about 1650 B.C., Mycenae became an important center of Greek culture. Mycenae was a wealthy and powerful city, located in the Peloponnesus. The people who lived there spoke a language that is similar to modern Greek. Other cities also began to blossom on the mainland. Thebes, Sparta, and Athens are just a few of the cities that were founded in the same era as Mycenae. Though the palaces of the Minoans on Crete were destroyed in about 1450 B.C., Minoan civilization had a great influence on its mainland neighbors in terms of art, religion, and culture.[3]

As their civilization spread, the people of Greece lived in towns that were independent of each other. The people who lived in what is known today as Greece were united by two factors: they spoke roughly the same language, and they thought of themselves as "Hellenes," or fellow descendants of Hellen, the legendary founder of the Greek people. (Today the modern Greek word for the country of Greece is *Hellas*.) There was no single ruler, and there were often wars between the different communities. It is important to remember that the people we call Greeks today were, at one time, not unified at all.

In the eleventh century B.C., an unknown enemy destroyed the ancient city of Troy, located in the western part of Asia Minor. It was against this city that the Greeks supposedly fought as a single group in order to rescue

Helen, the wife of Menelaus, the king of Sparta. Soon after this event, many major cities on the Greek mainland were destroyed. Later, Greeks blamed this massive destruction on an invading group of Greek-speakers whom they called the Dorians.

In about 800 B.C., the Greek alphabet was created, using the Phoenician alphabet as a model. This invention began a period of great political and commercial development on the Greek mainland and the surrounding islands. At that time, the various communities began to think of themselves as living in separate political entities known as city-states. The Greek word for city-state is *polis*.

In 508 B.C., Athens became the world's first democracy when free adult males were allowed to vote on matters concerning the city. The word *democracy* comes from the Greek word *democratia*, which means "ruled by the *demos*, or the people." It is important to note, however, that only citizens could vote in this democracy, and not everyone living in Athens was considered a citizen. At that time, many Athenian families owned slaves, who were often captives of war. Slaves were not considered citizens, and, therefore, not allowed to vote, and women held a nonvoting status as citizens.

During the rise of Athenian democracy during the sixth and fifth centuries B.C., great strides were made in the fields of philosophy, history, medicine, and the arts. It was a period of great development, especially in Athens, where some of the world's most influential thinkers could be found. This era is often referred to as the "Golden Age of Greece" or the "Golden Age of Pericles," referring to the ruler at the time.

In 338 B.C., Phillip II, a ruler from Macedonia, an area in the northern part of Greece, took control of most of the Greek mainland. Phillip and, after his death, his son,

Alexander, led military campaigns to build up their empire. At the height of his power, Alexander's empire stretched as far east as India. By late in the third century B.C., however, the Roman empire was beginning to gain strength, and by the middle of the second century B.C., Greece had come under Roman control completely. When Rome conquered Greece, the Romans adopted many of the customs, religious beliefs, and myths of their new subjects.

Literature

The Greek myths we are familiar with today are the product of generations of storytelling. Many were adaptations of stories that the Greeks gleaned from other cultures. Before about 800 B.C., when the Greek alphabet was developed, myths were passed down from one generation to the next by word of mouth. It was also through oral storytelling that myths and legends traveled from one part of Greece to the next, as well as to other parts of the world. However, after 800 B.C., stories began to be written down, including most of the tales that we now recognize as the basic core of Greek mythology.

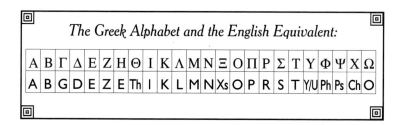

The Greek Alphabet and the English Equivalent:

A	B	Γ	Δ	E	Z	H	Θ	I	K	Λ	M	N	Ξ	O	Π	P	Σ	T	Y	Φ	Ψ	X	Ω
A	B	G	D	E	Z	E	Th	I	K	L	M	N	Xs	O	P	R	S	T	Y/U	Ph	Ps	Ch	O

Because the Greek alphabet is different from the one we use in English, scholars will differ in choosing the English equivalent for a Greek word. For example, the name of the god of fire may be spelled Hephaistos or Hephaestus, depending on the writer. In this book, we have tried to spell words and names so that they sound similar to their Greek equivalents but are also easy to read.

Sometime in the eighth century B.C., the poet Homer is thought to have composed *The Iliad* and *The Odyssey* (although many scholars debate his authorship). These two epic poems contain famous stories about legendary events in Greek history. *The Iliad* tells the story of the tenth year of the Trojan War, which may actually have taken place around 1250 B.C. when the real city of Troy was destroyed. *The Odyssey* recounts the adventures of Odysseus, a legendary ruler from Ithaca, a real island, located off the west coast of the Greek mainland. No one knows much about Homer. Legend has it that he was a blind poet who may have lived in Asia Minor or on Chios, one of the islands off the coast of Asia Minor. Because oral storytelling was such an important tradition before the advent of writing, Homer's stories may have been told for generations before they were ever written down.

Another important figure at this time was a poet known as Hesiod, who was born around 700 B.C. His two surviving poems are the *Theogony*, which tells the story of the mythic creation of the world, and *Works and Days*, which tells other important stories. These two works tell us a lot about the prevailing myths surrounding the various gods and goddesses in Greek legend and religion at this time.

During the time when democracy was developing in Athens, literature and the arts were also prospering. Theater was one of these arts. Three of Athens' greatest playwrights were Aeschylus, Sophocles, and Euripides. Many of the myths we know today come from their plays.

For scholars today, another important source of Greek myths is actually the work of Romans. When they conquered the Greeks, the Romans absorbed many aspects of Greek culture. The poet Ovid, who lived from around 43 B.C. to A.D. 17, was both a prolific writer and an influential figure in Rome. One of his most significant contributions to modern scholarship is his fifteen-volume work called *The Metamorphoses*, which retells the stories of many Greek myths. For centuries, this text has inspired other artists and poets.

Religion and Culture

The ancient Greeks were polytheistic, which means they believed in the existence of many gods and goddesses. A group, or collection, of gods and goddesses is called a pantheon, and the leader of the Greek pantheon was Zeus, the king of the gods and ruler of the sky. The Greeks believed that the gods had enormous power over the world and that they controlled nature in all its forms. The gods were often worshipped in temples erected in their honor. Most cities had a particular god or goddess whom they considered a special protector. Athens, for example, looked to the goddess Athena and the god Poseidon as its particular protectors.

The cities also held festivals in honor of individual gods at various times of the year. At many of these festivals, poets would dramatically recite the stories of the gods' adventures. One of the most famous festivals in the ancient Greek world was the festival in Athens honoring Dionysus, the god of wine. During the festivities, plays would be performed and judged in a competition, and it was during this festival that modern theater was born.

The worship of the gods often included a sacrifice. Usually, it was an animal, such as a goat, that was offered. The Greeks also believed in oracles, or prophets. At the temples of various gods, the priests, who could be either men or women, were often called upon to interpret omens, such as the sighting of a certain kind of bird or the appearance of some other natural event. One of the most famous oracles was located at Delphi where there were many important temples. People would travel from all over the Greek world to visit the temples and honor the gods.

The gods and goddesses were a major part of everyday life in ancient Greece, and each god had a particular role. Sometimes the gods had several jobs. Zeus, for example, the ruler of the sky and the leader of the gods, was also a protector of guests and travelers. Hera, Zeus's wife, was the goddess of marriage and childbirth. Athena was the protectress of Athens, but she was also the goddess of wisdom and war. Poseidon was another protector of Athens but, as the ruler of the sea, he was an important god for sailors and those who traveled by boat. Hephaestus was the god of fire, and he also served in the role of blacksmith for the gods.

The Greeks believed that the gods lived on Mount Olympus, a real mountain in the central part of Greece called Thessaly. However, according to Greek tradition, the gods could leave their mountain and go anywhere. Myths and legends often told of the gods taking on human forms and walking among the people.

Within the pantheon, the gods often married each other, and some of them had more than one spouse or partner at a time. Sometimes the gods married their siblings, parents, or children. The god Zeus, for example, had many partners other than his wife, Hera, who was also his sister. Throughout the various mythological stories, Zeus appears to have had more than one hundred fifteen mistresses![4] The gods and goddesses were often paired in different ways because the myths were always developing and being retold. As people began to believe different things about different gods, they associated the gods with one another in new ways. Zeus, as the most powerful god, often seemed to be a part of all the other gods' lives.

Though the gods had affairs and children by many different partners, real Greek marriage customs were very strict. Women were married at a young age, often to men who were much older; and the marriages, at least in Athens, were usually arranged by families based on economic needs and political tactics, rather than affection. It was not socially acceptable for women to have romantic relationships with men outside of marriage, regardless of what the gods and goddesses were thought to do.

In addition to being part of the plays and poems recited at festivals, the stories of the gods and goddesses were also frequently told at home and in schools. The following myths, therefore, were an important part of the everyday social and religious life of the ancient Greeks.

1

CREATION

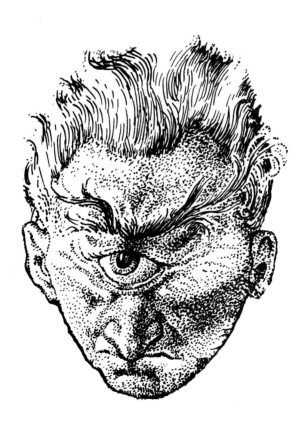

INTRODUCTION

Most cultures have myths that help to explain the creation of the universe and the beginning of time. Because the origin of the universe is unknown, each culture has tried its best to make sense of this mystery.

An important Greek creation story comes to us through Hesiod's poem, the *Theogony*. The *Theogony* seems to have been the earliest surviving literary version of the creation of the earth and the birth of the gods in the Greek pantheon. In the *Theogony*, Hesiod appeals to the Muses, the patronesses of the arts, for inspiration and wisdom as he begins to relate the succession of gods and the story of creation. Invoking the Muses' help was a common way for poets to begin their work:

> Tell how at the first gods and earth came to be, and rivers, and the boundless sea with its raging swell, and the gleaming stars, and the wide heaven above, and the gods who were born of them, givers of good things, and how they divided their wealth, and how they shared their honors amongst them. . . . These things declare to me from the beginning, you Muses who dwell in the house of Olympus, and tell me which of them first came to be.[1]

In this creation myth, the development of the earth coincides with a rise in the powers of the ruling gods. The first entity that ruled the universe was called Chaos. The word *chaos* literally means a wide-open space, but it can also describe a deep cavern or chasm. The goddess Gaia's name literally means "earth" or "land." The name of Gaia's child and husband, Uranus, means "sky" or "heaven." There is a close connection between these god-like figures and the physical elements suggested by their names. In this sense, then, Gaia is both a goddess and the earth itself, and, similarly, Uranus is both a god and the heavens.

CREATION

Before there was land or sea, people or gods, nothing existed, except Chaos. Chaos was a space of neither order nor disorder. During Chaos's reign, there was no organization of any kind in the universe. There was no sun or moon. There were no mountains or rivers, nor any such features on earth. In fact, there was no earth at all. It was a period of vast emptiness. Even time did not exist. Eventually, Chaos divided itself into the earth, the sky, and the sea. When the division was complete, everything was peaceful and perfect.

After Chaos divided into the earth, sky, and sea, one goddess came into being without being born to any mother. Her name was Gaia, which means earth, and she took control over the earth as it took shape. Mountains became separate from the plains, and rivers and oceans were formed. Like an artist at a canvas, Gaia was busy creating a beautiful masterpiece. Soon, however, the goddess began to long for children to help populate and rule this magnificent new world.

Gaia's desire for children was so great that eventually she became pregnant by herself. The child she bore was named Uranus, and he became the ruler of the sky. In every way, Uranus was the equal of his mother, and soon Gaia and Uranus had children together.

Gaia's first three children were monsters, called the Hundred-handed Ones. They were giants, and each had fifty heads and a hundred hands. Although Gaia loved her children and was proud of them, Uranus was afraid that someday one of these children would overthrow him. Because of this fear, Uranus hated the children and forced them back into Gaia's womb.

After the hundred-handed monsters had been born and were pushed back into their mother's womb, Gaia gave birth to three more monstrous children. These were giants called the Cyclopes. Each had but a single eye, which was positioned directly in the middle of his forehead. Although they were frightening to look at, these young gods were exceedingly strong, and they were excellent craftsmen who made thunder and lightning for

their mother to use as tools and weapons. Unfortunately, Uranus was afraid of these children, too. So, in order to get rid of them, Uranus tied the Cyclopes up and threw them into a deep cavern called Tartarus. Tartarus was far, far away, and Uranus felt safe in believing that he would never see these monster-children again.

Saddened by the loss of the Hundred-handed Ones and the Cyclopes, and angry at the cruel Uranus, Gaia gave birth to a third group of children. These were called the Titans, and there were twelve of them—six goddesses and six gods. They were very different from their older siblings. The Titans were beings with human characteristics, and they were not monsters at all. The goddesses' names were Tethys, Theia, Mnemosyne, Rhea, Themis, and Phoebe.

The gods' names were Oceanus, Hyperion, Iapetus, Cronus, Crius, and Coeus.

Uranus was still afraid that one day one of his children would overthrow him. Because of this fear, he pushed the Titans back into Gaia's womb alongside their siblings, the Hundred-handed Ones. Gaia was enraged by Uranus's refusal to allow her children to live freely. She desperately wanted her children to live without restraints and to enjoy the world. Finally, she came up with a plan that would allow her children to be born into the world and remain there.

Gaia could speak to the children in her cavernous womb, and she had no trouble convincing them to help with her plan. Cronus, the youngest of the twelve Titans, was the most eager to help his mother. So, the two set out to trick Uranus and free the Titans and the Hundred-handed Ones from their mother's prison-like womb.

Cronus and Gaia waited for the perfect opportunity to enact their plan. Finally, one night, when Uranus came to Gaia's bed, Cronus crept out of Gaia's womb and stabbed his cruel father with a sickle, a curved knife used to harvest crops. As Uranus lay dying, his fears of being overthrown by one of his children having come true, Uranus leaned forward and cursed his son: "Cronus," he pronounced, gasping for breath, "it will come to pass that one of your children will do to you what you have just done to me." Then, with a final shudder, Uranus died, a look of anger and betrayal in his eyes.

After Uranus died, Gaia and her children felt free for the first time. The Titans and the Hundred-handed Ones were reborn from their mother's womb, and the Cyclopes were freed from Tartarus. All of Gaia's children decided to make Cronus their king. Cronus married his sister, the Titan named Rhea, and ruled over the universe for a long, peaceful time.

QUESTIONS AND ANSWERS

Q: *What existed before the earth was formed?*

A: Chaos is the name for the empty space that existed before the earth, the sky, and the sea were formed. Chaos was a space of neither order nor disorder.

Q: *Who was Gaia?*

A: Gaia was the first goddess to exist after the division of Chaos. Her name means "earth," and she gave the earth all its attributes.

Q: *How was Uranus related to Gaia?*

A: Uranus was Gaia's son, who became the ruler of the sky. Uranus was also the father of Gaia's other children. He did not have a father himself.

Q: *Why did Uranus hate all of the children Gaia bore him?*

A: He was afraid that one day, one of his children would overthrow him.

Q: *What was unique about Gaia's first children, and what happened to them?*

A: Gaia's first children were monsters. Each Hundred-handed One had fifty heads and a hundred hands. Uranus pushed these three children back into their mother's womb.

Q: *Who were Gaia's second children, and what happened to them?*

A: Three Cyclopes were born after their hundred-handed siblings. Each Cyclopes had a single eye set in the middle of his forehead. The Cyclopes were strong, and they were excellent craftsmen. Uranus locked them in a deep cavern called Tartarus.

Q: Who were Gaia's third set of children, and what happened to them?

A: Gaia's youngest children were the Titans who had characteristics similar to humans. Uranus pushed these twelve children back into Gaia's womb with the Hundred-handed Ones.

Q: Who was Cronus, and how did he save the Titans?

A: Cronus was the youngest of all Gaia's children, one of the Titans. He killed his father, Uranus, with a sickle. By committing the act, Cronus was able to set the gods free from their mother's womb.

Q: What was Uranus's final curse?

A: As he was dying, Uranus cursed Cronus, predicting that one day, one of Cronus's children would rise up and overthrow him, just as Cronus had overthrown Uranus.

EXPERT COMMENTARY

The myths of the gods and goddesses were as important in Greek society as religion itself. Most people were familiar with these stories, and many could even recite them in their entirety. Scholar Lucilla Burn notes:

> Greek myths permeated Greek life, private and public. In the well-documented society of Athens in the fifth century B.C., for example, it is clear that a major part of education was learning and reciting epic poems on heroic subjects. Guests at drinking parties might entertain each other by reciting stories from myths, or they might listen to a professional performer, who would sing of the deeds of heroes while accompanying himself on the lyre. Private homes contained pottery vessels decorated with scenes from the adventures of the gods and heroes; these same vessels accompanied their owners to the grave. Scenes of myth could also be woven into fine textiles.[2]

Although there are many stories about the first generation of gods, in many ways they still remain a mystery to modern scholars. The author of *The Uses of Greek Mythology*, Ken Dowden, explains:

> The Titans are a puzzle. We do not know where their name comes from and individually they are a rag-bag of persons, abstractions and even monsters. Anyone born of Heaven and Earth, rather than from [Cronus] and Rhea like the Olympian gods, must apparently on that account be a "Titan."[3]

The story of the first immortal generation may have been symbolic of some kind of agricultural or fertility activity among the early Greeks. In his book *Greek Mythology*, John Pinsent suggests:

> For Uranus is cut with the sickle, an instrument which however well suited for the purpose may legitimately suggest that the story has been also influenced by stories of the annual sacrifice of the corn or its representative.[4]

2

THE WAR BETWEEN THE TITANS AND THE OLYMPIANS

INTRODUCTION

Sometimes real places are named in a myth. Mount Olympus, for example, is a real mountain in the central part of Greece, not far from the Aegean Sea. When Mount Olympus is referred to in myths, however, it becomes more than a mere geographical site. It becomes the home of the Olympians, the generation of gods who succeeded the Titans. These two generations of gods eventually became rivals, fighting a great war for power over the universe. The winners claimed Mount Olympus as their home. Although there is an actual mountain, in these stories, Mount Olympus is a mythical place that humans cannot visit. It is a place outside real time and space.

Mount Olympus is not the same as Olympia, a town in the western part of the Peloponnesus. Like Mount Olympus, Olympia was named for the Olympian gods. There were important shrines in Olympia, an area which was settled even as early as the third millennium B.C.[1] The first Olympic Games were probably held there sometime in the eighth century B.C., although they seem to have been a carryover from an earlier tradition.[2] The purpose of the games was thought to be a kind of reenactment of the rivalry between the Olympian gods and the Titans, and a commemoration of the triumph of the Olympian gods over the Titans in their war. During the Olympic Games, quarrels were supposed to be set aside in order that athletes be allowed to take part in peaceful competition.

Although people did not believe that the gods took an interest in their individual lives, they often went to the temples to ask the gods for insight and help. Olympia was an important site in this respect. According to Mark P. O. Morford and Robert J. Lenardon, professors of Greek mythology, the gods were thought to send humans messages in the form of natural signs or omens, which were then interpreted by priests at the shrines of the various gods:

> The traditional methods for eliciting a response from [Zeus] were by the observation and interpretation of omens, for example, the rustling of leaves, the sound of the wind in the branches of his sacred oaks, the call of doves, and the condition of burnt offerings. At Olympia inquiries were usually confined to the chances of the competitors at the games.[3]

The story about the war between the Titans and the Olympians is a vital one in Greek mythology. In this myth, we learn that even the evolution of the immortal gods was wrought with conflict. Nothing came easy for the Olympian gods, but, although the odds were stacked against them, they never gave up. As was also true in the daily lives of the Greek people, perseverance was an important quality—so important that it was central to their stories and their religious beliefs.

THE WAR BETWEEN THE TITANS AND THE OLYMPIANS

After the death of Uranus, the world was at peace again. Cronus, the king of the Titans, and Rhea, his most noble sister and wife, had matters well in hand. Unfortunately, the curse of his father, Uranus, haunted Cronus day and night. Was it possible that one day he, too, would have a child who would overthrow him?

One day, Rhea announced that she was going to have a baby, but her husband was not happy. Cronus was so afraid that history would repeat itself that he did, in fact, manage to repeat history. Like his father before him, Cronus reasoned that if he could keep his children from growing up, none could ever become strong enough to overpower him. So, when Rhea gave birth to her first child, Cronus quickly grabbed it and swallowed it whole. Rhea was both horrified and saddened at the loss of her firstborn child. In a similar manner, Cronus swallowed all of the next four children that she gave birth to, and Rhea vowed to get them back, any way she could.

By the time Rhea discovered that she was pregnant for the sixth time, she had figured out a plan to trick her husband and save the newborn child from being swallowed whole. So, when it was nearly time for her to give birth, Rhea pretended to have her baby. She took a large stone and wrapped it in a baby's blanket. When Cronus came to gobble down the newborn child, Rhea gave him the wrapped-up stone. Quickly, Cronus swallowed the stone, just as he had swallowed the other children. In fact, Cronus's focus on swallowing the newborn god was so great that he did not even realize that he had been tricked.

Later, when the time came for Rhea actually to have her child, she fled to the island of Crete. There, away from the glaring eyes of her husband, Rhea secretly gave birth to a son, whom she named Zeus. He was a beautiful and strong baby, and Rhea knew that when he grew up, he would be a truly powerful god. Rhea realized that she could not return home to her husband with the child. Cronus would only try to destroy the newborn god, as he had done with the others. Therefore, for his protection, Rhea left Zeus to grow up secretly on Crete where he was suckled by a goat and raised by minor native deities called nymphs. While Zeus was a child, Cronus never suspected that he had been tricked and that he actually had a stone resting solidly in his stomach.

When he had grown into a young man, Zeus left Crete to join his mother. Rhea arranged for Zeus to become a servant to his father. Cronus did not know that his new servant was actually his son. One day, Zeus brought his father a cup of wine, which Cronus drank quickly. This cup of wine contained a special potion, which made Cronus throw up. Cronus was so violently ill that he even threw up the stone wrapped in a blanket. Then he threw up all of the children he had swallowed before. The children emerged from their father's stomach as fully grown adults. Their names were Poseidon, Hades, Hera, Demeter, and Hestia. These were Zeus's brothers and sisters, and they were all

glad to see each other in the light of day. Although they were happy to be free, the six siblings knew they must do something immediately, or their father would swallow them all over again. Quickly, they ran away while their father continued to moan and clutch his stomach.

This young generation of gods fled to Mount Olympus to escape their irate father, and because they claimed Mount Olympus as their home, the young gods were called the Olympians. After they had fled to safety, the Olympians quickly formed a plan. At once, they declared war on Cronus and many of the other Titans. The young gods wanted to rule the world in their father's place. Yet their struggle had a dual purpose: while they were fighting for control over the earth, they were also fighting for their lives, since they knew that Cronus would swallow them again if he ever got the chance.

And so a great war began. At first, it seemed likely that the Titans would be victorious and remain in control of the earth. The young Olympian gods felt outnumbered and overpowered. The tide began to turn, however, when a few Titans changed sides and fought with Zeus and his siblings. Prometheus, the son of the Titans Themis and Iapetus, was one who switched his allegiance. Prometheus's name means "one who thinks ahead," and with his ability to see the future he could foresee that the Titans would lose the battle against the Olympian gods. Prometheus and his brother Epimetheus refused to fight against the Olympians because of this foresight.

The Cyclopes and the Hundred-handed Ones also joined the Olympians in their fight against the Titans. They did not feel bound to the Titans, and they believed that the Olympian gods would rule with steadier hands. Zeus asked the one-eyed Cyclopes to make weapons for his army, and these skilled craftsmen made a special weapon for each of the gods. For Zeus, the leader, the Cyclopes fashioned a special thunderbolt, which could be thrown long distances with great force. For Poseidon, they created a magnificent trident, or three-pronged spear, which could defeat any enemy. Finally, knowing that resistance came in many forms, the Cyclopes made Hades a magic helmet that could make him invisible, even to the immortal eyes of Cronus and the other Titans.

The war between the Titans and the Olympians was terrible. With the help of the Hundred-handed Ones, who fought bravely without ever tiring, the Olympians soon forced the Titans to surrender. After the Titans had given up, Zeus challenged Cronus to a wrestling match. The winner would control Mount Olympus, to which the Titans were still laying claim. After beating Cronus three times, Zeus declared the Olympian gods to be the winners.

After the war, the Olympians sent most of the Titans to Tartarus to be locked up for eternity. The victors built a bronze gate over the mouth of the cavern, and the Hundred-handed Ones were placed outside as guards. Atlas, another child of Iapetus and Themis, who had led the Titans into battle, received a special punishment. He was forced to hold the world on his back for all eternity. This turned out to be a far more challenging task than imprisonment in Tartarus.

Cronus, the former ruler of the universe, was not sent to Tartarus with his siblings. Though Cronus had swallowed his children whole, Zeus and the other Olympians did not want to destroy him in revenge. Instead, Cronus was sent away to live on the Island of the Dead, where he stayed forever. Although originally he had wanted to destroy the Olympian gods, Cronus, once defeated and exiled, sent dreams to his son Zeus to guide him from afar.

After all the punishments were handed out, Zeus, Hades, and Poseidon made a bet to determine who would rule each part of the world. Hades became the lord of the dead and the Underworld, which was sometimes called Hades in his honor. Poseidon gained control of the seas and all the waters on earth. Zeus became the lord of the sky; and since the sky covers everything on earth, he became the king, or father, of the gods.

After these important decisions were made, the other Olympian gods were also given jobs. Demeter became the goddess of agriculture and of all growing things. Hestia became the goddess of the hearth, or fireplace, and the home. Hera, too, protected the home and became the goddess of marriage and childbirth after she married her brother, Zeus.

Once the Olympians had defeated the Titans and taken on their new roles, they, too, had children. Some of these gods were born under rather extraordinary circumstances. Athena, for example, was born out of the side of Zeus's head. She became the goddess of wisdom and the protector of Athens. Hera became pregnant on her own and gave birth to Hephaestus. Hephaestus was the god of fire and became the blacksmith of the gods. Ares was the child of Hera and Zeus, and he became the god of war.

Apollo, the god of light and music, and his twin sister, Artemis, the maiden goddess of the hunt, were the children of Leto, who was the daughter of the Titans Phoebe and Coeus. The goddess of love and beauty, Aphrodite, had an unusual birth: she was born out of the waves of the sea.

Hermes was another son of Zeus. His mother was Maia, one of the daughters of Atlas. Hermes grew very quickly, and he was swift-footed, even as a baby. Later, he became the official messenger of the gods because he was so fast. He was often depicted with wings on his hat and sandals, and because he was always moving about, he was a particular protector of travelers.

These gods and others lived on Mount Olympus after their victory over the Titans. From the height of this great mountain, the new rulers could look down on all of Greece and keep watch over the world, for the control of which they had fought so hard.

QUESTIONS AND ANSWERS

Q: *Why was Cronus afraid of his children?*

A: Cronus feared that one of his children would rise up and overthrow him, just as he had done to his own father. Uranus had cursed Cronus, predicting that history would repeat itself.

Q: *How did Cronus get rid of his children?*

A: He swallowed them whole.

Q: *Why and how did Rhea trick her husband?*

A: Rhea was angry and upset at Cronus's practice of devouring their children, so she planned a trick for him. When it came time for Cronus to grab the sixth newborn child, Rhea gave him a large stone wrapped in a baby's blanket. Because he did not expect the trick, Cronus swallowed the stone, blanket and all.

Q: *What kind of weapons did the Cyclopes make for the Olympian gods?*

A: Some of the weapons that the Cyclopes made were a thunderbolt for Zeus, a trident for Poseidon, and a magic helmet for Hades.

Q: *How did the Olympian gods punish the Titans?*

A: The Olympian gods locked most of them away in the cavern called Tartarus. The Hundred-handed Ones stood guard over this prison. The Olympians also set Atlas to work holding the world on his shoulders. He received this punishment because he had led the Titans in battle.

Q: *What happened to Cronus?*

A: The Olympians did not utterly destroy Cronus. Instead, they sent him to the Island of the Dead where he lived for eternity.

Q: *How did Cronus wind up helping his son Zeus?*

A: From his exile on the Island of the Dead, Cronus sent dreams of advice to his son.

Q: *How did Zeus, Hades, and Poseidon divide up the control of the universe?*

A: Zeus became the king, or father, of the gods and ruled the sky. Hades became the ruler of the Underworld, or the land of the dead. Poseidon gained control of the seas and all the waters on the earth. They determined these roles through a bet.

EXPERT COMMENTARY

Many words in English can be traced to the Greek language. However, because many Greek words sound alike to the foreign ear, sometimes they are easily confused. Scholar Richmond Y. Hathorn explains:

> Even in pre-classical times the name of Cronus seems to have been confused with the Greek word *chronos*, "time." Perhaps the god's connection with the year-cycle contributed to the confusion. The result was a spate [stream] of poetical and philosophical speculation. Cronus swallowing his children was not merely, on the agricultural level, a picture of the fertile earth engulfing the seeds, but a statement of the grim truth that Time devours everything it produces.[4]

The names of places were often taken from the names of the gods. Author John Pinsent writes:

> Atlas stood in the west in the sea that is beyond Ocean, and is called Atlantic after him. . . .[5]

The scholars Morford and Lenardon suggest the blending, or assimilation, of different sets of beliefs and traditions in shaping the myths:

> When the inhabitants of Crete began to build their great civilization and empire (ca. 3000), the religion they developed (insofar as we can ascertain) was Mediterranean in character, looking back to earlier Eastern concepts of a mother-goddess. The northern invaders who entered the peninsula of Greece (ca. 2000), bringing with them an early form of Greek and their own gods (chief of whom was Zeus), built a significant Mycenaean civilization on the mainland, but it was strongly influenced by the older, more sophisticated power of Crete. The myth of the birth of Zeus reads very much like an attempt to link by geography and genealogy the religion and deities of both cultures.[6]

3

PROMETHEUS AND EARTH'S FIRST INHABITANTS

INTRODUCTION

Many of the myths show the gods acting in response to something a human has said or done. However, in their daily lives, and in the practice of ancient Greek religion, the people remained distinctly aloof from the gods. In fact, the people did not believe the gods loved them—and, in return, they did not feel compelled to love the gods back. The people simply accepted the gods as all powerful and understood that their power was never to be questioned.[1] Some of the stories about the creation of mankind show the gulf that lay between the mortals and their heavenly counterparts.

One of these stories involves Prometheus and his brother Epimetheus. These brothers were sons of Titans who had crossed sides and fought against their relatives in the war between the Titans and the Olympians. Prometheus's name means "the one who thinks ahead," and he behaved as his name suggests, often making wise and anticipatory decisions. Epimetheus's name, on the other hand, means "the one who thinks afterwards," and he, too, behaved according to his name.

Prometheus was an important figure in the mythical development of the earth and the creation of human beings. The Greeks believed it was Prometheus who had taught them how to survive in the newly created world. However, in trying to help the humans, Prometheus got into trouble with the gods. Eventually, the gods punished Prometheus by tying him to a rock on the top of a mountain. The Caucasus Mountains that are mentioned in the story are real, geographical mountains, located to the east of the Black Sea, far away from the Greek mainland.

PROMETHEUS AND EARTH'S FIRST INHABITANTS

After the world was created and the gods had fought their wars, the land that lay below Mount Olympus remained unpopulated, even though Gaia, the first goddess, had long yearned to make creatures to inhabit the earth. Finally, Zeus decided it was time.

It was a good time to be created. No monsters roamed the earth, and the world was at peace. Zeus began to make creatures to populate this beautiful world. However, just as he was beginning, he was called away to settle a matter dividing his fellow Olympians. He decided to appoint Prometheus and Epimetheus, sons of Titans who had fought with the Olympians, to continue the project of creating earth's first inhabitants.

Although the brothers were Titans by birth, they had sided with the Olympians in the war against Cronus and the other Titans because, blessed with the gift of being able to see the future, Prometheus had foreseen the Olympian victory. Prometheus was the more sensible of the two brothers, and he always planned ahead. Epimetheus, on the other hand, always meant well, but he never planned ahead. Epimetheus never thought about the consequences of his actions until after he had completed them.

Zeus had chosen these brothers for the project of creating the first people and animals on earth because Prometheus was an excellent potter and sculptor. Prometheus could make just about anything, and he had a good imagination. Epimetheus was invited to work on the project because he was always eager to help his brother.

Because Zeus had only just started to make the various earth creatures, the brothers had a lot of work ahead of them. After using clay to sculpt the new creatures into their basic shapes, Prometheus went to Athena, the goddess of wisdom, for advice on how to complete the work. Epimetheus stayed behind to give the unfinished creations their final distinguishing features.

Athena's advice was simple. She told Prometheus that since the creatures were already composed of earth and water, having been fashioned from clay, the only element lacking for life was air. So, Athena advised Prometheus to hold each of the newly shaped creatures up to the sky. When the wind blew into them, she promised, they would breathe and be truly alive.

Meanwhile, Epimetheus continued to work. He enjoyed showing off his creative powers and granted a wide variety of interesting physical attributes to all the different creatures. Epimetheus gave some of them fur and hair, which would protect them from the elements. He gave others teeth and claws so that they could easily collect and eat food. In addition, he gave some of the creatures strength and speed.

When Prometheus returned from his talk with Athena, he found that once again, his brother had acted before thinking. Epimetheus had been so excited about designing the new animals and so generous with his creative powers that he had completely forgotten to save any special gifts for the human beings. By the time the sculptor had gotten around to the humans, he had run out of ideas. They were left weak and defenseless, and they would have remained so forever if Prometheus had not stepped in. Once he realized that his brother had created a species unable to stand on its own in the new world, Prometheus set forth to fix the mistake and make human beings strong and capable of surviving among earth's other inhabitants.

First, Prometheus decided to help the humans stand upright like the gods. He turned their heads upward to the sky. This adjustment gave them the power to reason. Then he raced to the heavens where he lit a torch, using the fire of the sun. He used this fire to light up the new creatures' powers of thought and speech. These special powers helped set the humans apart from the other animals.

At first, the gods approved of Prometheus's work. They were glad to see that there was a species on earth that had the ability to think and speak. But Prometheus was still not satisfied. He saw that Epimetheus's poor planning had left the new humans physically weak compared to the other inhabitants of the earth. They were hungry, sad, and scared. Finally, to help the humans, Prometheus left Mount Olympus and went to live on earth with the people, in order to teach them the skills they would need to survive in the new world.

First, Prometheus showed the humans how to build houses so they would not have to live in caves. Then he taught them how to read, and how to write numbers and letters. He helped the people learn how to tame animals and how to sail on the seas. He showed them how to heal themselves when they were sick. After he had shown the people how to foretell the future and recognize omens by looking at the way birds flew, some of the other gods became impressed by the new people. They decided to help, too. Demeter, the Olympian earth goddess, taught the new race of creatures about edible plants. With this help, the humans had better access to food, and they began to prosper and live happily for the first time.

Although some of the gods were excited about the development of the humans, other gods were beginning to worry that the humans were becoming too powerful. However, despite the growing concerns of his fellow gods, Prometheus was so pleased with his creations that he decided to help the humans even more. Until this time, humans were only allowed to slaughter other animals if they were performing a sacrifice to the gods. They ate only the plants that Demeter instructed them to eat. Prometheus could see that the humans would probably need to eat the meat of other animals to survive.

So Prometheus came up with a plan. First, he cut up an ox, as if for a sacrifice. Then, he divided the sections into two piles. In one pile, Prometheus wrapped up the bones of the ox and hid them under shiny morsels of fat. This pile looked like the more attractive offering in a sacrifice. For the other pile, Prometheus took the lean meat and other edible parts of the ox and wrapped them in hide, topping the pile with entrails to make the offering look disgusting.

Once this was done, Prometheus asked Zeus to choose one of the two piles and keep it as the sacrificial offering; the humans would take whichever pile Zeus rejected. Not knowing that the good meat was actually hidden beneath the hide and entrails, Zeus chose the pile shimmering with fat. Once Zeus had made his choice, he had to stick with it, even after he discovered that he had chosen a pile with no edible meat in it. From then on, people offered the fat and bones of animals to the gods, and they kept the savory parts of the animals for themselves. Zeus was outraged that Prometheus had tricked him, but he decided to save his revenge for later.

This was not the only trick Prometheus played on the Olympian gods for the sake of the humans. Since the new race of creatures had no fur, they were often cold, and even though they were now allowed to eat meat, they had no way to cook it. Human beings did not know about fire or how to control it because, until this point, fire belonged only to the gods. Prometheus decided to change things. He went up to heaven and secretly stole fire from the gods. Hiding the fire inside the stalk of a fennel plant, Prometheus brought it back to the people on earth. Then he taught the people how to cook grains and meat, and how to keep fire burning so that it would always be available. Prometheus also showed the humans how they could use fire to forge metal, just as Hephaestus, the god of fire and the forge, was doing on Mount Olympus.

Prometheus did all these things to help the humans because he wanted them to survive in the world now populated by other, more physically powerful creatures. Unfortunately, Prometheus's efforts angered some of the other gods. The new people were getting too powerful and too smart. Zeus thought they needed to be stopped before they believed their own powers were supreme and they no longer heeded the authority of the gods. Furthermore, Zeus was furious with Prometheus for all his tricks.

To punish Prometheus for tricking the king of the gods and for making humans so powerful, Zeus had him captured and chained to a rock on the crest of one of the Caucasus Mountains. Every day, an enormous eagle came to the spot where Prometheus was tied. The eagle was fierce and relentless, and each day it swooped down and pecked away at Prometheus's liver, devouring the greater part of it. Because Prometheus was immortal, his liver grew back every night, and he never died. Despite this

intense torture, he endured the punishment for thirty years until Hercules came and freed him.

Unfortunately, punishing only Prometheus did not satisfy Zeus's desire for revenge. The king of the gods had other plans that would affect the entire human race, and it was a punishment that would last forever.

QUESTIONS AND ANSWERS

Q: *What are the meanings of the names Prometheus and Epimetheus?*

A: Prometheus means "the one who thinks ahead." Epimetheus means "the one who thinks afterwards."

Q: *What job were Prometheus and Epimetheus given, and why were they chosen for this honor?*

A: Prometheus and Epimetheus were given the job of finishing the creation of earth's first inhabitants. They were chosen for the job because Prometheus was an excellent potter and sculptor, and he had a good imagination. Epimetheus was reliable and could be counted on to help his brother.

Q: *What element did Athena advise Prometheus to add to the creatures?*

A: Athena explained that since Zeus had used clay when he began to make the creatures, they were already made of earth and water, two essential elements. She told Prometheus that the only element the creatures lacked was air; when the creatures were held up in the wind, they would breathe and become alive.

Q: *How did Epimetheus fail to think ahead in completing earth's creatures?*

A: Epimetheus gave all the qualities of power and strength to other animals. Some of them were given wings, claws, teeth, and fur for protection and to help them survive. Humans were left defenseless, with no special gifts.

Q: *How did Prometheus help make humans capable of surviving in the new world?*

A: First he helped humans stand upright so they could turn their heads up toward the sky. He gave humans souls and the power to think and speak. Prometheus also taught humans skills like building, reading and writing, and medicine. Prometheus tricked the other gods into allowing humans to eat meat. Finally, he gave humans fire and showed them how to use it.

Q: *Why were the gods angry at Prometheus for giving humans fire?*

A: The gods feared humans would become too wise and too powerful. They were afraid that the people might be able to compete with the gods.

Q: *How did Zeus punish Prometheus?*

A: He chained Prometheus to the top of one of the Caucasus Mountains, where every day an eagle devoured most of his liver.

EXPERT COMMENTARY

Zeus's method of punishing Prometheus for helping the humans seems excessively cruel to our modern sensibilities. However, Barry B. Powell, a professor at the University of Wisconsin, explains that it would have been a punishment familiar to people in ancient Greek society:

> This method of punishment actually existed: Vicious criminals were taken to the boundaries of a territory, stripped naked, nailed to a post, and allowed to die miserably, when eaters of carrion [dead meat] consumed their flesh. . . .[2]

Although Hesiod and many other poets had told this story earlier, the myth of Prometheus and his punishment was immortalized in the fifth century B.C. by the Athenian dramatist, Aeschylus, in his play *Prometheus Bound*. Through these early writers, Prometheus became known as mankind's greatest helper. Even today, he is often referred to as the symbolic father of creativity. Mark P. O. Morford and Robert J. Lenardon write:

> Fundamental to both Hesiod and Aeschylus is the conception of Zeus as the oppressor of humankind and Prometheus as its benefactor. In Aeschylus the clash of divine wills echoes triumphantly through the ages. His portrait, more than any other, offers the towering image of Prometheus as the Titan, the bringer of fire, the vehement and weariless champion against oppression, the mighty symbol for art, literature, and music of all time.[3]

4

PANDORA

INTRODUCTION

In ancient Athenian society, women lived very difficult lives. They had no economic or political independence, and even in the home, women were treated as inferior and often lived in a special part of the house known as the women's quarters. Girls were not formally educated like their brothers. They lived in their father's house until they married as young teenagers, at which time they moved to their husband's home. They did not speak to men outside the intimate circle of family members. When Athens became a democracy at the start of the fifth century B.C., women could not vote.

Despite the fact that Athenian women were not offered equal opportunities in their society, women often play important, and sometimes menacing, roles in Greek mythology. It is a contradiction then that, in both myth and reality, women were expected to be virtuous and good; at the same time, however, it was commonly believed that they were devious and wicked beneath their noble façade.

In mythology, Pandora was the first human woman, and her story may represent the contradictory issues associated with Greek women. Hephaestus, the god of fire and the forge, created Pandora at Zeus's command. Zeus intended her to be a form of punishment for the newly created human males. Zeus and some of the other gods wanted to put the humans back in their place after their powers had been so greatly enhanced by Prometheus. To achieve the gods' ends, Pandora is endowed with many gifts, among them great beauty and charm. The gods also give her a gift that will ultimately set free all the evils in the world—an ornate box, or a jar, depending on the version of the tale. Despite her own good intentions, the first female causes much grief and pain for mankind.

The story of Pandora and her intriguing but destructive box comes to us through Hesiod's *Theogony*. Pandora is a figure who has been interpreted in many different ways. Much of the contradiction surrounding this famous mythological character is thought to come from Hesiod's understanding, or misunderstanding, of her name. Mythology scholar Richmond Y. Hathorn explains, "The name *Pandora* does not mean 'she who was endowed with all gifts' [as in Hesiod's version of the story] but rather 'she who is giver of all,' and as such it was an epithet [name] of the earth-goddess."[1]

PANDORA

Zeus was furious. Prometheus had tricked him, and the king of the gods wanted revenge. He also wanted to remind the humans that they would never be as powerful as the gods.

So far, there were only men in the human population. Women did not yet exist, although certainly there were female gods, or goddesses. Introducing women to the human race was part of Zeus's plan for revenge. First, Zeus went to the forge of Hephaestus and asked him to design a human being that would be female. Carefully, Zeus explained that she should be like the men on earth, yet somehow slightly different.

Hephaestus was happy to do Zeus a favor, and he went right to work. The god of fire and the forge was a very talented smith. Everything he made was beautiful, and his new creation was no different. When he was finished with the creature he showed his work to Zeus, who was very pleased with the results. The new creature was named Pandora. She was human, but she was clearly a woman. She was very beautiful and looked like a goddess. She had long flowing hair, flawless skin, and bright shining eyes. She was as graceful as a soft breeze, and she had a smile precious to see. Zeus hoped that her beauty would make the male humans accept and trust her.

After Hephaestus had put the finishing touches on the first human woman, the gods showered her with many gifts, including golden-threaded clothes, shining jewelry, and fragrant smelling flowers. Among the gifts was a box that was covered with jewels, intricate carvings, and decorations. The box was very pretty, and Pandora was certain that such a beautiful object must surely contain something of equal magnificence. However, the gods had given Pandora the beautiful box on one condition: She could look at it as much as she liked, but she was never to open it. Pandora did not understand the reasoning behind this rule, but because the box was so pretty, she agreed to follow the warning of the gods.

Soon Pandora went to live on earth with the other humans. When she got there, she met Epimetheus who was living among the humans with his brother Prometheus. Epimetheus was overwhelmed by Pandora's dazzling beauty, and he fell in love with her instantly. Prometheus, aware of his brother's infatuation with Pandora, became suspicious that Zeus and the other Olympians were planning a trick. Prometheus warned his brother to be wary of any gift sent to earth by the Olympian gods. As usual, Epimetheus did not listen to his brother. He was very much in love with Pandora, and despite his brother's warning, he married the wonderful new creature and brought her to his home. Epimetheus never thought to ask his new bride about the beautiful box she always carried with her.

The couple lived very happily after their marriage. Every day, Pandora would lovingly admire her beautiful box, but she obeyed the order of the gods and never opened it. Soon, however, looking at the box was not enough. Her curiosity became stronger and stronger, and finally one day she could no longer resist the urge to open the box, regardless of the consequences.

When Pandora opened the box and discovered what was hidden inside its beautiful exterior, she knew at once that Zeus's revenge had been accomplished. Inside the magnificent box were all the evil spirits known to the gods. Now that the lid was open, they all quickly flew out. Sorrow, hunger, anger, disease, madness, and a hundred other horrible conditions filled Pandora's room and, like smoke, they escaped out into the world to plague mankind for the rest of time. As the evils swarmed around her, Pandora became frightened. As quickly as she could, she slammed shut the lid of the box, but Pandora realized that it was too late to regret not having obeyed the gods. Their revenge was final. However, Pandora noticed that one spirit still remained in her box. This was the spirit of hope.

Soon, when they felt the effects of the various plagues and evil spirits that had flown out from Pandora's box, the people on earth understood that their time of peace had ended. The people recognized the power of the gods' revenge, and understood that forces existed that were stronger than their own modest powers. From that time on, the people vowed to do their best to keep from angering the gods any further and were comforted by the fact that hope was safe in Pandora's box. The knowledge that hope had not been destroyed gave the people faith that peace would return some day.

QUESTIONS AND ANSWERS

Q: *Why did Zeus want revenge against the humans?*
A: He feared that with Prometheus's help the people on earth had become too smart and powerful.

Q: *Who was Pandora and how was she created?*
A: Pandora was the world's first woman. Hephaestus, the blacksmith god and expert craftsman, made her at the request of Zeus. Zeus wanted to use Pandora to punish the humans who were, until that point, all men.

Q: *What did the gods give Pandora?*
A: They gave her many wonderful gifts, like beauty, grace, lavish clothes, and fragrant flowers. They also gave her a beautiful box covered with jewels and intricate carvings. It was filled with every conceivable kind of evil.

Q: *What warning did the gods give Pandora?*
A: The gods warned her never to open the box they had given her.

Q: *Why did Pandora open the box?*
A: Her curiosity had grown too strong.

Q: *What happened when Pandora opened the box?*
A: Evils of every kind, like sorrow, hunger, anger, pain, disease, and madness flew out of the box and into the world, where they plagued mankind for all time.

Q: *What remained in the box?*
A: Hope remained in the box.

EXPERT COMMENTARY

In the story of Pandora, human curiosity is a key ingredient. Pandora's box has come to represent the temptations of curious minds, but there is also much confusion regarding the contents of the box. Morford and Lenardon write:

> Details in the story of Pandora are disturbing in their tantalizing ambiguity [lack of clarity]. What is Hope doing in the jar [or box] along with countless evils? If it is a good, it is a curious inclusion. If it too is an evil, why is it stopped at the rim? What then is its precise nature, whether a blessing or a curse? Is Hope the one thing that enables human beings to survive the terrors of this life and inspires them with lofty ambition? Yet is it also by its very character delusive and blind, luring them on to prolong their misery?[2]

The story of Pandora and her role in the gods' revenge against mankind suggests that women were considered a mixed blessing in ancient Greek society. Barry B. Powell recognizes this apparent misogyny, or hatred of women, as it is presented in Hesiod's version of the story:

> Modern readers are struck by the virulence [extreme bitterness] of Hesiod's attack on women, although it is not different in message from the biblical story of Eve. The roots of misogyny are varied and not easily understood, especially in an age when women's rights are a prominent political issue. . . . Among the Greeks, however, misogyny seems to be based not so much on primitive magical terror, or economic resentment as in Hesiod's surly complaint, as on a male resentment of the institution of monogamy [marriage with one partner] itself. Greek myth is obsessed with hostile relations between the sexes, especially between married couples. In reading such passages we need to remember that, with only minor exceptions, ancient literature was composed by males for males in an environment ruled by males (as was the Bible).[3]

5

DEMETER AND PERSEPHONE

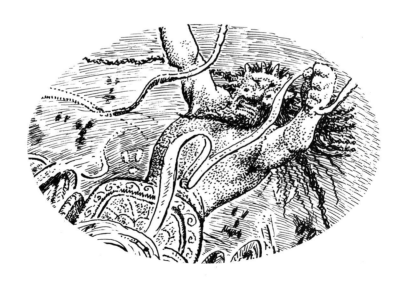

INTRODUCTION

Demeter, the daughter of the Titans Cronus and Rhea, was one of the first Olympian gods. After the war between the Olympians and the Titans, Demeter became an important goddess of agriculture. Her name meant "earth mother" or "grain mother." With Zeus, her brother, Demeter had a daughter named Persephone who was also called Kore, which means "maiden." The people of ancient Greece prayed to Demeter for healthy crops and abundant harvests. She was often associated with Dionysus, the god of wine, who was also worshipped at harvest time.

People thought that it was Demeter who allowed vegetation to grow in the spring, summer, and part of the fall, and to die in the winter. When the ground was fertile and the grains grew successfully, Demeter seemed like a kind goddess; but when winter came, or when there was a drought, people thought she must be angry or upset. Her followers prayed that she would always be happy and therefore kind to the earth.

In one of the most important myths about Demeter, her beloved daughter Persephone is abducted, or kidnapped, by Hades, the lord of the Underworld. Hades, another Olympian god, was an important figure in Greek mythology: He was the ruler of the dead and of unseen ghosts. During the war against the Titans, the Cyclopes had given Hades a helmet that made him invisible; even his name seems to come from the Greek word meaning "the unseen." Although Hades played an extremely significant role in Greek religion, he was considered an unlucky god to invoke. Thus, not many religious ceremonies were dedicated to him, and he had few individual followers.

As the ruler of the world under the earth, Hades was

thought to give the earth richness in the form of crops; at the same time, he was respected and feared as the governor of the dead. Because of his connection to the earth, Hades is appropriately connected to Demeter and Persephone, two goddesses who were thought to control the fertility of the land and the abundance of the harvest.

Until the fourth century A.D., the greatest temples to Demeter could be found in Eleusis, a town located near the sea not far from Athens. Every autumn, there were festivals to honor Demeter in Eleusis, and they were some of the most famous celebrations in the ancient world. Unfortunately, no one knows exactly what went on at these festivals because they were kept secret. Today the festivals are known as the Eleusinian Mysteries. The people who took part in the ceremonies, called "initiates," were sworn to secrecy about the sacred rites that were performed. Many scholars believe that the main purpose of the Eleusinian Mysteries was to thank the goddess for the harvest and to pray to her for continued bounty.[1]

The infertility of winter and its resulting hardships were undoubtedly a great mystery to the ancient Greeks. The myth of Demeter and her daughter Persephone is one way that the people of ancient Greece came to explain this inhospitable season.

DEMETER AND PERSEPHONE

Demeter and Zeus had a daughter named Persephone. With two powerful gods as parents, it is not surprising that the little girl grew up to be a beautiful maiden. Her mother loved the child more than anything else in the world and cringed at the idea of ever being apart from her.

After she had grown up and become a young woman, Persephone's beauty caught the eye of Hades, the ruler of the Underworld. Hades fell in love at the very first sight of her. He knew he wanted to marry no one else. Overcome with love, Hades went to Zeus, his brother and Persephone's father. He said, "Brother, I am in love with your daughter, Persephone. Let me have your consent to marry her. I will make her the queen of my kingdom in the Underworld."

Zeus thought that Hades would be a good husband for Persephone. Hades was a fair and powerful god. However, Zeus also knew that Demeter would never allow her daughter to marry Hades and go to live far away in the Underworld. If the maiden were to marry Hades, the mother and daughter would be separated indefinitely. Zeus also knew that Demeter, the goddess of growth and fertility, would never wish her daughter to live in the stark, bleak world of the dead where nothing ever grew. Although he was king of the gods, Zeus was wary of Demeter's powerful influence over all the things that blossomed on earth. He did not want to upset her.

Zeus pondered his dilemma for quite some time. He wanted to please his brother and allow the marriage, but he did not wish to cause a conflict with Demeter. Finally, Zeus found a clever way to grant his brother's request without actually saying so. Carefully wording his response, Zeus said, "Brother, I cannot approve of a marriage between you and Persephone."

Zeus was telling Hades that although he could not officially approve the marriage, he was not forbidding it

either. Hades understood Zeus's intention. He realized that Zeus was encouraging him to mary Persephone without her parents' blessing. Hades felt certain that if he acted in this prescribed manner, Zeus would not be angry with him. He understood that Zeus was just trying to keep the peace by officially saying neither yes nor no to the marriage proposal. Satisfied, Hades returned to the Underworld to plan the details of exactly how he would go about kidnapping Persephone.

One day, soon after Hades's meeting with Zeus, Persephone went to pick wildflowers with her friends near the town of Eleusis. No one expected trouble in the peaceful meadow, and the girls were looking forward to

an amusing and relaxing day. After a little while, Persephone wandered away from her friends, picking flowers here and there and adding them to her basket.

In a small wooded glen near the meadow, out of sight and earshot of her friends, Persephone spotted a beautiful narcissus that she thought would make a lovely addition to the bouquet she was making for her mother. Dreamily, Persephone knelt to pick the flower. She was surprised to find that its roots were so deep that she could not wrench it out of the ground. Suddenly, as she tugged mightily on the flower, a huge hole opened up in the middle of the glen. The god of the Underworld raced out of the chasm, the roaring noise of his chariot filling the air. Quickly, Hades grasped the frightened maiden by the wrist and pulled her up beside him onto his chariot. Racing off to the Underworld, Persephone cried out in fear to her mother and her friends.

Up on Mount Olympus, Demeter heard her daughter's terror-filled cries. She hurried to the area where the girls had been playing. Persephone's friends had been frightened when their friend failed to return, but no one could tell where she had gone. Distraught, Demeter roamed the earth for nine days and nine nights, searching in vain for her beloved daughter.

On the tenth day, Demeter met Hecate, a goddess who lived in a cave near the spot where Persephone and her friends had been playing. Hecate had indeed heard Persephone's cries for help, but alas, she had not seen what had happened to the girl. Though she could offer no new information about Persephone's disappearance, Hecate offered to help Demeter look for her daughter. Together, the two goddesses set out on their search.

The next morning, the goddesses came upon Helius, the god of the sun. Helius could see everything from his lofty perch in the sky, so Demeter begged him for information about her daughter's disappearance. Helius pitied Demeter and promised to tell her everything he knew. He confessed that he had seen Hades kidnap Persephone, and that the girl had cried uncontrollably when she was made Hades's bride. Helius was sorry for Demeter's loss, but he hurried to point out that as ruler of the Underworld, Hades exerted power over a third of the world. He tried to console Demeter by saying, "I know you are sad to be separated from your daughter, but the powerful Hades is a good match for the fair Persephone."

However, Demeter would not be consoled. She cried, "My beautiful daughter? Why should she be taken so far away among the sunless dead?" Thinking about her daughter's situation all over again, Demeter became so upset that she left Hecate and Helius and began to shun her fellow immortals.

Soon Demeter took to wandering the earth in the guise of a mortal woman. She allowed the grain harvest to fail and the fields to become parched. She was so transformed by her grief that no one could recognize her. She looked like a gnarled, old woman, as sad and weak as the parched and unyielding fields that were beginning to patch the earth.

After wandering for many months, Demeter came again to the town of Eleusis where she stopped to rest by a well. While she was sitting in the shade of an olive tree, four beautiful princesses came to draw water. They were the daughters of Celeus, the king of Eleusis, and all four were kind and well-mannered. When they saw Demeter, they pitied her because she looked so sad and weary. They had no idea that she was really a goddess. Trying to help the old woman, the girls asked if she would be interested in being a nurse to their baby brother, Demophoon. Demeter gladly accepted this offer.

When Demeter entered the palace, her golden hair had turn to gray, her skin was wrinkled and loose, and all her inner radiance was hidden beneath a dark robe. Nevertheless, the princesses' mother, Queen Metanira, sensed that the new nurse was not an ordinary old woman. The queen noticed a special glow about the newcomer, despite her dark robe and sad face. Metanira offered Demeter her best chair and asked one of the servants to bring some sweet wine, but Demeter, too sad to accept comfort, refused the chair and the wine. Instead, she sat on a low stool and drank only water mixed with barley mead. Then Demeter asked to see the child for whom she would be caring. When Demeter first took the baby Demophoon in her arms, he smiled and gurgled. Queen Metanira was glad to see that her newborn son was comfortable in the arms of his new nurse.

Demeter was happy watching over the young prince. She began to love the child so much that, eventually, she decided to make him immortal. By doing so, Demeter hoped to thank the royal family for their kindness and, at the same time, to relieve some of the sadness of losing her own child. So each night, after the family was asleep, Demeter lathered the boy with ambrosia, an ointment of the gods. When he was well oiled, she placed him in the heart of the hearth's fire to burn away all traces of his mortality. Though the baby was in the fire, Demeter watched him intently, and the flames never hurt him.

The ambrosia treatment worked wonders, and the baby grew stronger and healthier every day. The royal family was amazed at the baby's rapid development. Demophoon was growing much faster than a normal child. Soon, however, Queen Metanira became suspicious of her son's remarkable growth. One night she did not go to bed. Instead, she hid, hoping to see what the nurse was doing each night to her youngest child. When Metanira peeked into Demeter's room, she was shocked at what she saw. There was the nurse, turning her baby in the fire like a pig on a spit!

Metanira screamed at the sight. Interrupted at her magic, the goddess angrily jerked the child from the fire and threw him to the ground where he began to cry— unhurt but frightened. Hearing his wife's scream, King Celeus came running into the room, just in time to see the old nurse transform herself into a towering, beautiful goddess. As her form changed, a blaze of light burst forth and filled all the gloomy corners of the palace room.

Though she was furious with Metanira for the interruption, Demeter's anger quickly turned to sadness. She decided not to punish the family for their reaction. She had, after all, loved the baby, and although he could never become immortal without continuing the ambrosia treatments, he could still be honored, since a goddess had been his nurse.

Demeter told the king and queen to have the people of Eleusis build a temple in her honor. While it was being built, she told the townspeople how to grow corn and how to perform special ceremonies at her temple. In this way, the town continued to appease and pay tribute to the inconsolable goddess, whose grief once again became focused on her lost daughter.

When the temple at Eleusis was completed, Demeter went to live there, far from Mount Olympus and the other gods and goddesses. Sadly, she sat silently in her temple for an entire year. While she sat, no crops grew, and the people became hungrier with every passing day. Soon it seemed like every living thing on earth was in danger of starving.

Zeus feared that Demeter's mourning was becoming destructive. He begged her to end the famine, but Demeter repeatedly refused the request. She said she would never grant her life-giving power to the earth so long as Persephone remained so far away in the Underworld. Finally, Zeus realized that Hades would have to give up his bride so that the world could be healed. With a heavy heart, Zeus sent Hermes, the official messenger of the gods, to the Underworld to deliver a message to Hades.

When Hermes reached the Underworld, he found Hades and his bride sitting side by side on their thrones. Persephone looked miserable. She was weeping because she missed her mother and the world above. When she heard Hermes's message from Zeus, she cried out in joy. Hades knew that he had no choice but to obey Zeus and let Persephone go home to her mother. He begged his wife not to think of him harshly. Hades said, "My beloved wife, remember that here you are the queen, the most powerful woman of all. As the queen of the Underworld, you even have power over the living, because you have control over what happens to people when they die. Because of this, you have the power to be merciful, which is the greatest gift of all. Do not think ill of me or this kingdom when you are far away from here."

Reluctantly, Hades prepared to let Persephone go, but before she left, he gave her four pomegranate seeds to eat. Hades knew, although his wife did not, that if she ate anything from the world of the dead, she would have to return to his kingdom someday.

Having eaten the seeds, Persephone rode happily out of the Underworld with Hermes. When their chariot finally reached Eleusis, Persephone joyfully embraced her mother. The mother and daughter laughed and cried, and talked as they had before. Finally, Demeter asked her daughter if she had eaten anything during her stay in the Underworld. Persephone replied, "Mother, what a strange question. All I ate was four pomegranate seeds. Why should that matter?"

Demeter became so upset by this news that she took her daughter directly to Zeus to discuss what could be done. On the way to Mount Olympus, Demeter explained to Persephone that because she had eaten food from the Underworld—the seeds of the pomegranate—she would have to return there. That rule was unbreakable.

Zeus had witnessed the happiness of mother and daughter when they were reunited, and now he could see the unbearable sadness in their eyes at the thought of having to part again. Nevertheless, Zeus had to respect the rules of the universe. Therefore, to follow the rules, the king of the gods decreed that Persephone must return to the Underworld. However, Zeus offered a compromise: instead of returning permanently to live in the Underworld, Persephone need only live there for four months out of the year, one month for each pomegranate seed she had eaten. Appeased by Zeus's compromise, Demeter allowed the crops on earth to grow again.

From that time on, mother and daughter spent two thirds of the year together. During their time together, the earth bloomed and the crops flourished. But when Persephone returned each year to spend four months with Hades in the Underworld, the earth became as cold as ice while Demeter mourned for her daughter's lost company. Then, every spring, when Persephone returned to her mother, the world would become green again in celebration of their joyous reunion.

QUESTIONS AND ANSWERS

Q: *What was Demeter's role as a goddess?*

A: She was the goddess of agriculture. Demeter was responsible for providing healthy crops, fertility, and bountiful harvests.

Q: *Who was Hades?*

A: Hades was the god who ruled the Underworld, or the world of the dead.

Q: *Why did Zeus refuse to give his consent for Hades to marry Persephone?*

A: Zeus did not want to anger Demeter, Persephone's mother and the goddess of agriculture, who could cause the earth to become barren.

Q: *Why did Hades kidnap Persephone?*

A: He wanted to marry her. He knew that Demeter would never allow her daughter to marry someone who lived in the Underworld. He also realized that although Zeus would not grant his consent for Hades to marry Persephone, Zeus did not precisely forbid the marriage. Without her parents' official consent, Hades knew he had no choice but to kidnap Persephone.

Q: *What did Persephone eat while in the Underworld?*

A: She ate four pomegranate seeds.

Q: *What is the significance of the four seeds?*

A: The four seeds came from the Underworld. Once she had eaten food from the Underworld, Persephone would be bound to return there.

Q: What compromise did Zeus make for Demeter and Persephone, and why did he make it?

A: Instead of forcing Persephone to return permanently to Hades and the Underworld, Zeus allowed Persephone to spend two thirds of the year on earth with her mother. Persephone had to return to the Underworld for four months out of every year, one month for each seed she had eaten. Zeus allowed this compromise because he wanted to keep Demeter happy. He knew that if she remained sad, the earth would dry up and become barren.

Q: How does the myth of Demeter and Persephone help to explain the seasons?

A: Each year, when Persephone went to the Underworld, Demeter grew sad. She did not let anything grow on earth, and winter set in. Then, when Persephone left the Underworld to return to her mother, the earth became fertile again, and spring returned.

EXPERT COMMENTARY

The story of Demeter and Persephone is often considered to be the basis for many other myths, including some stories in modern Christianity. Michael Grant, a respected historian, writes:

> The tale of Demeter and Persephone, perhaps more than any other classical myth, has embodied and directed man's accumulated thoughts about being born and dying. It anticipates both Easter (in which life and death co-exist) and Christmas (the time of annual rebirth and hope).[2]

This myth and the celebrations of the Eleusinian Mysteries, provide the English language with some important words. Professor Barry B. Powell explains:

> The word *mystery*, which has entered our language from this Eleusinian cult to Demeter, comes from the Greek [word] *mystês* (plural *mystai*) meaning "one who closes his eyes," in order to enter the temple or during the sacred rites. From the Latin translation of the word, *initiatus*, comes our word *initiate*, literally, "one who has gone in," that is, into the temple of Demeter to participate in the secret ritual.[3]

The myth of Demeter and Persephone is also significant to modern scholars because it helps to illustrate the fate of women during this period in Greece. Powell writes:

> Persephone's fate resembles that of Greek girls who, at age fourteen, were married to war-hardened men twice their age, whom they scarcely knew. . . . Demeter's fate is also typical of many Greek women. As Demeter lost a child to Hades, the lord of death, so did many lose a child to war or disease. In the myth we see that Demeter's loss causes her first to grieve and to rage, before she finally accepts that, although things have changed, the world will go on. Many Greek women would easily have identified with this sequence of emotions.[4]

6

DIONYSUS AND HIS FOLLOWERS

INTRODUCTION

Although Athens may have been the most important, ancient Greece had many other cities that were significant to the development of culture and religion. Thebes, for example, was the major cultural and military center of Boeotia, an area to the northwest of Athens on the Greek mainland. According to legend, the hero Cadmus had come to the land of Boeotia by following a cow there. (The word *Boeotia* is related to the Greek word for cow.) He had sown the teeth of a dragon into the earth like seeds, and after battling the race of men who had sprung out of the ground from these seeds, Cadmus took control of the area and built the city of Thebes. Cadmus and his wife Harmony, the daughter of Ares and Aphrodite, had four daughters: Autonoe, Ino, Agave, and Semele. The character Cadmus is believed to have originated in Eastern religion, and the story about the foundation of Thebes may reflect the influence of a foreign group on the area.[1]

Thebes was thought to be the birthplace of a very significant member of the Greek pantheon. Dionysus was the son of Zeus, the ruler of the Olympian gods, and Semele, one of Cadmus's daughters. Dionysus, the god of wine, was also called Bacchus. He was an important god of agriculture, and he was often closely associated with other earth gods, such as Demeter. Because he was affiliated with grapes and wine, the Greeks believed that Dionysus could control a person's state of mind, in the same way that alcohol does, and he is often connected to scenes of madness or various forms of wild behavior.

During the fifth and sixth centuries B.C., theater as we know it was born during the Athenian festivals dedicated to Dionysus. These festivals placed a heavy emphasis on the recitation of poetry, and the theatrical forms of comedy and tragedy that we know today developed out of the performance of this poetry. The most famous playwrights of the time were Aeschylus, Sophocles, and Euripides, who often based their plays on the prominent myths and historical events of the day. This story about Dionysus, and the development of his importance, has been passed down to us through the play *The Bacchae* by Euripides.

In the story, Zeus makes a promise and seals it by pledging an oath on the name of the River Styx. This is the mythological river that must be crossed in order to enter the Underworld. Any promise sworn upon it could never be broken, not even by a god.

DIONYSUS AND HIS FOLLOWERS

Semele's father was Cadmus, king of Thebes. She lived a happy and luxurious life in the palace, along with her sisters Autonoe, Ino, and Agave. As the girls grew older, everyone remarked on their outstanding beauty. Life seemed perfect for these lovely princesses, until the day Semele fell in love with a tall, handsome stranger.

Caught up in her new romance, Semele ignored the fact that she did not know much about her lover. She kept him a secret from her family and friends, and although her sisters noticed a new radiance about Semele, none suspected her frequent absences.

Semele had no idea that her secret lover was actually Zeus, the king of the gods, who was visiting her in the form of a mortal man. Zeus was very much in love with the beautiful, quiet, and somewhat solitary princess, but he could not visit her in his true godlike state. If he were to reveal his true self, Semele would die, since no human could look on an immortal in his or her true form without being consumed by the immortal's power. Therefore, when a god wished to show himself to a mortal, he needed to cloak his glory. However, after Semele and Zeus had continued their love affair for some time, Zeus finally decided to reveal his true identity to Semele. Although she was shocked, the princess believed her lover.

Even though Zeus was in love with Semele, he was, in fact, already married to Hera, the queen of the gods. When she learned of her husband's affair with Semele, Hera became enraged with jealousy. In fact, Zeus often pursued other women, both mortal and immortal, and although she was used to her husband's affairs, Hera still always reacted with the same intensity. She often took out her revenge on her husband's various accomplices.

This time, Hera, disguised as a servant, paid a visit to Semele's bedchamber. With mock sympathy, Hera told the girl that she knew all about the secret romance. Somehow she convinced the princess that it would be wise for her to behold her lover in his true form. Semele had just discovered that she was pregnant, and although she trusted her lover, she now became persuaded to be certain about the identity of her unborn child's father.

So Semele sent the servant out of the room and awaited the arrival of her lover. When Zeus entered the room through a door from the garden, Semele jumped up and threw her arms around his neck. "My love," she said, "my servant knows all about us. We must be very careful or my father will discover our affair! But this is not my only news. Darling, I am going to have a child. Swear to me that you will grant me the favor I am about to ask you."

Zeus was surprised at the princess's ardent tone of voice, but because he was so much in love with her, he agreed and said, "I swear on the River Styx in Hades that I will do whatever you ask of me."

Semele took her lover's hand and led him into the room. Sitting down, she begged to see him in his true form. Zeus was caught off-guard and did not know what to do about this new dilemma. He knew that Semele would not be able to look at him without dying, and he did not want to hurt her. But the god had also made an unbreakable promise, for any promise sworn on the River Styx must be fulfilled, and now he could not refuse her request. Though Zeus tried to explain the consequences to Semele, the princess insisted that, although she truly loved him, she still needed proof of his identity.

Therefore, reluctantly, Zeus kept his word. As he began to transform, the room filled with light, and flames shot out from his immortal body. Semele screamed as the sight of her lover burned into her eyes. Then, consumed by the fire of Zeus's immortality, her own body was engulfed in flames. Just before she died, Zeus snatched Semele's unborn baby from her womb. Quickly, he sewed the baby into his thigh to keep it safe from harm. Then Zeus wept for his love, and he left the Theban palace in the same secret manner by which he had come.

When nine months had fully passed, Semele's child was born out of Zeus's thigh. The king of the gods named his son Dionysus, and he asked some nymphs to raise the baby and keep him a safe distance away from Queen Hera who was still angry at Zeus for his affair with Semele.

Many years later, after Dionysus had grown up, he bade a tearful farewell to the nymphs who had mothered him and set off to travel the world, slowly making his way toward Thebes. He was a handsome young man with long flowing hair that fell in waves about his shoulders. He wore clothes made out of the skins of animals, and often he looked like he would be more comfortable in the wilds of the forest than in the cities and towns that he visited. As the young god wandered, he showed the Greeks how to grow grapes and how to use the grapes to make wine. He was often followed and worshipped by groups of wild-looking women called *Bacchae* or bacchantes. These women also

wore clothes made from the skins of animals, and they usually had flowers or leaves scattered in their hair. Often the bacchantes would sing and dance like untamed animals in their rituals of worship, and they caused quite an uproar wherever they visited.

After many years of travel, Dionysus finally arrived in his mother's hometown, and he was shocked at the poor reception he received. The people of Thebes did not believe that Dionysus was a god, nor did they believe he was Semele's lost son. Dionysus also learned that his mother's memory had been dishonored by the people of Thebes. The Thebans considered Semele to have been a disrespectful daughter; they disapproved of her secret affair and felt she had received a just punishment in her death! Dionysus was furious at the Theban people for both their disbelief of his immortality and their cruel treatment of his mother's memory.

At this time, the king of Thebes was Dionysus's cousin Pentheus, the son of Semele's sister, Agave. Like the other Thebans, Pentheus did not believe that Dionysus was a god, nor would he recognize him as his cousin. Pentheus thought that this stranger was merely a troublemaker whose wild and unruly followers were disturbing the peace of his orderly city. Angrily, Pentheus commanded his guards to arrest Dionysus and his disciples.

Although Dionysus was, in fact, enraged by Pentheus's behavior, the god went to prison peacefully. However, extraordinary things began to happen at the palace prison. The guards were amazed when they realized that it was impossible to lock up their peculiar prisoner. No matter how many times they worked the locks attached to them, the chains on Dionysus's wrists always fell to the ground, and the doors of his jail cell refused to stay closed. Then, suddenly, a huge earthquake rocked the city of Thebes, flattening both the palace and the prison to the ground. Many Thebans came to realize that this devastation must have been the work of an angry god. Despite these strange events, Pentheus refused to believe that Dionysus possessed any supernatural powers, even after the prisoner had walked out of the rubble of the prison without a scratch on his body.

Many Theban women, however, became convinced of Dionysus's powers, and after the earthquake, they joined Dionysus's followers. After dressing in animal skins, the women went to the hills outside Thebes where they cavorted like animals, jumping and dancing in praise of Dionysus, whom they now recognized as a god.

Soon, a messenger came to Pentheus to tell him that his mother, Agave, and his aunts were among the *Bacchae* dancing in the hills. The messenger also told Pentheus that guards had tried to talk to Agave and the other women, but when they had approached, the women chased the men away. The guard added that the women had torn the woods apart with their bare hands and ruined all the villages in their path with their wild revelry.

Pentheus was furious at this news! He paced in front of his crumbling palace, fuming. "My own mother!" he cried. "Acting like one of those crazy *Bacchae*! Whatever will happen next?"

As Pentheus grew visibly more and more upset, Dionysus approached, already planning his revenge. Pentheus still did not believe that Dionysus was a god, but soon he fell into a trance and agreed with everything Dionysus said to him, no matter how strange.

First, Dionysus convinced Pentheus that he needed to climb the hill and see for himself how the women were behaving. Only then would Pentheus be able to figure out a way to make them stop their outrageous behavior.

Still in a trance, Pentheus begged Dionysus to help him find a disguise so that the women on the hill would not recognize him. Then Dionysus dressed King Pentheus in a long, flowing wig and a wild, multicolored dress. Under Dionysus's spell, Pentheus thought he looked quite dashing when, in fact, he looked very silly.

Finally, Dionysus led the king to the hill where the *Bacchae* were celebrating. Once they reached the top of the hill, Dionysus convinced the king to climb a tree to get a better look at the scene. Then, when Pentheus had settled himself in the tree, Dionysus disappeared. The king was surprised that Dionysus would leave him so suddenly, but he was confident that the women could not see him hiding in the tree.

Unfortunately for Pentheus, Dionysus had put the women in a trance as well. Thus, when they looked up at the tree, they did not see Pentheus hiding there but a mountain lion readying for attack. Terrified at the sight of what she thought was a vicious, man-eating creature, Agave shouted, "Kill the lion!"

Like animals stalking their prey, the women attacked Pentheus and pulled him from the tree. Though he begged for mercy, the women could not understand him since his words sounded like the growls of a wild lion, not like cries for help from their own king.

Dionysus had endowed the women with superhuman strength, and now, with their bare hands, the women tore Pentheus to shreds. Then, still in a trance, the women marched back to Thebes. In tribute to their proud victory, Agave led the march, parading the head of the victim above her like a trophy. When the women entered the city carrying Pentheus's head before them, the people of Thebes were so horrified that they stood in silence as the shocking parade passed by.

When the marchers reached the grounds of the palace ruins, Agave called out to her father, Cadmus, to show off their prize. When Cadmus saw what Agave held in her hands, his face paled, and he began to weep. Holding the head of her victim high above her, Agave said, "Father, why do you weep? Look how I have killed a mountain lion! Look how strong and brave your daughter is! Why are you not proud?"

Weeping for his dead grandson, and for his daughter who loved her son Pentheus more than anyone in the world, Cadmus said, "Dear Agave, look again at what prize you have been blessed with, and then you will understand why I am weeping."

Cadmus's sad words broke Agave's trance, and when she looked again at the head in her hands, her proud laughter quickly turned to terror. She saw that she had killed her own son! Falling to the ground, Agave wept, finally coming to understand the powers of the god Dionysus, whom her family had so vilely offended by their disbelief.

QUESTIONS AND ANSWERS

Q: *Who were Dionysus's parents?*

A: Dionysus was the child of Zeus, the king of the gods, and Semele, the daughter of King Cadmus of Thebes.

Q: *How did Dionysus's mother, Semele, die?*

A: Because she was mortal, Semele could not look at Zeus unless he was disguised. When she persuaded Zeus to reveal himself in his true form, Semele was unable to withstand the power of the god's immortality, and she was burned to ashes.

Q: *How did Zeus save the baby Semele was carrying?*

A: As Semele's body was engulfed in flames, Zeus took the unborn baby from her womb and sewed it into his thigh. Later, the baby was reborn out of Zeus's thigh.

Q: *Why did Dionysus become angry with the people of Thebes?*

A: The Thebans did not respect the memory of his mother, Semele, nor did they respect his godlike powers and nature.

Q: *Why did Pentheus arrest Dionysus?*

A: Pentheus thought the young visitor was a trouble-maker, not a god. Pentheus thought Dionysus and his followers were disturbing the peace of the city.

Q: *Why did Agave kill her son, Pentheus?*

A: Under a spell induced by Dionysus, Agave mistook Pentheus for a mountain lion. When she came out of the trance, Agave was shocked and horrified by what she had done.

EXPERT COMMENTARY

Dionysus was often thought to be a late addition to the Greek pantheon, or set of gods. As was true in this story, he was sometimes only reluctantly accepted, and often he was viewed as an outsider. He was known as the god of wine and of altered states. It is important to note that people believed that Dionysus had the power not only to cause the intoxication of the body, as through the consumption of wine, but also the intoxication of the spirit, as through ecstatic or frenzied behavior. Richmond Y. Hathorn writes:

> In his myths Dionysus invades from without because it was his nature as a god to apparently invade the individual from without: of all deities he was the one who most character-istically "possessed" his devotee; he "filled the devotee with the god," sometimes through the medium of wine, more often directly, since he was essentially the wild spirit of intoxicated joy that thrills throughout the whole realm of nature.[2]

Dionysus was also known in Greece by the name Bacchus, and it is from this name that we have derived the term *bacchanalia*, which is a riotous celebration or scene of revelry. The people who worshipped Dionysus were considered wild and out of control. In fact and in fiction, the supporters of Dionysus were associated with nature and insanity. In *Mythology, An Illustrated Guide,* editor Roy Willis explains:

> The mythical male followers of [Dionysus] were the satyrs, creatures who were part man and part goat with horses' tails. His female followers, both in myth and reality, were called Bacchants ("women of Bacchus") or maenads ("mad women").[3]

The worship of Dionysus is also connected to the birth and development of Western theater. Professor Barry B. Powell writes:

> Dionysus also played an important role in Greek culture through his association with the theater. Many of the best-known Greek myths are preserved as the plots of tragedies performed in his honor. Beginning in the sixth century B.C., tragedies were performed at a spring festival of Dionysus in Athens known as the Lenea. . . . Others were performed at the more important City Dionysia [or festivals to Dionysus], probably reorganized sometime in the middle of the sixth century B.C. . . . Some elements in Greek drama seem to be traceable to the cult of Dionysus, in whose honor these festivals were held, but more than a hundred years of intensive scholarship have been unable to clarify the precise relationship between the cult and Greek drama.[4]

7

BAUCIS AND
PHILEMON

INTRODUCTION

Greece has always had a close and tumultuous relationship with its neighbors to the east. In the ancient world, the civilizations in Asia Minor had an important role in the development of Greek religion and culture. The groups of people in Asia Minor, a great part of which is now Turkey, and the people of Greece often had much in common. Due to trade and travel, they had many opportunities to share myths and religious beliefs.

The story of Baucis and Philemon probably crossed the cultural divide. The myth was written down by the Roman poet, Ovid. Phrygia, the land where Baucis and Philemon live, was located in Asia Minor, but in this story, Zeus and Hermes, gods who are Greek in origin, visit the area as if it were just another part of their Greek landscape.

Because travel was so central to the lives of the ancient Greeks, there were many customs related to the treatment of guests and travelers. For example, it was considered an honor to have a guest in one's home. All guests were to be respected and treated kindly, even if they were strangers. Zeus was the particular protector of guests, and Hermes, the fleet-footed messenger of the gods, was considered to be a protector of travelers and the god of the highway.

In the myths and folktales of many cultures, a disguised king or god sometimes visits common people. These stories remind people always to offer kindness to strangers, since the true identity of a stranger can never be known. The story of Baucis and Philemon demonstrates the importance of the custom of respecting visitors.

BAUCIS AND PHILEMON

Baucis and Philemon lived in Phrygia, a part of Asia Minor. They had been married for many years, and although they were very poor, they were happy and loved each other dearly. Their farm was small, and they could grow only enough to feed themselves. Sometimes conditions made it difficult to coax any crops out of the land, so they often relied on the eggs of the single goose that lived on the farm. The goose not only laid eggs, but it acted like a watchdog, protecting the couple's meager possessions.

One day, Zeus and Hermes decided to visit Phrygia. Zeus, the protector of guests, wanted to see if the people in Phrygia were being kind to visitors. Zeus and Hermes wore ragged clothes so that no one would recognize them. They knew that as gods they would be treated royally, but they wanted to see how they would be welcomed as ordinary travelers.

Thus disguised, the gods went from house to house in Phrygia. At the door of each house the ragged strangers asked the owners if they could rest by the fireplace and have something to eat and drink. But each door was slammed rudely in their faces. After this had happened many times, Zeus began to worry. He turned to Hermes and asked, "How can anyone travel in such an inhospitable country where everyone seems so rude and disrespectful? Are there no people in Phrygia who are kind to strangers? Travelers far from home should not have to go hungry. I wonder how these rude people would feel if they were treated the same way they have been treating us?"

Hermes had no ready answer for Zeus, and the pair trudged along. Finally, after knocking on hundreds of doors and being refused hospitality at each one, the disguised gods found themselves before a hut that was smaller and more rundown than any of the houses they had yet visited. The house was situated near the bottom of a tall hill, and although the farm around the house was small, the grounds were well-tended. When the strangers knocked on the door of the modest hut, a ragged couple appeared. Immediately and with open arms, they invited the strangers into their home. Ducking under the low doorway, the disguised gods entered into the small but spotless single room.

The couple's names were Baucis and Philemon. Baucis was a small woman with graying hair, a sweet face, and a friendly smile; and her husband, Philemon, was hard-working and strong despite his years. They were kind and happily went to work preparing a meal and trying to make their guests feel comfortable.

Baucis and Philemon asked neither the visitors' names nor their origins; the couple understood that it was up to the visitors to offer this information only if they so chose. With sincere attention to their visitors' comfort, the couple invited their guests to sit near the warm hearth, and Baucis threw a thin pillow over the single hard bench. Then Baucis heated up the fire and began to boil water. While she cooked the evening meal, Baucis spoke happily with the guests. "We are so glad to have you with us," she said.

"We do not have much, my Philemon and I, but we are happy to share whatever we have with our friends." As she said this, her husband smiled and nodded in agreement.

Finally, the meager meal was ready. Baucis propped up their rickety table with a broken dish and served her guests. Philemon made sure that the guests had whatever they might need. The couple were so busy enjoying their company that nothing seemed unusual. Gradually, however, Philemon and Baucis both noticed that although they had already used up their small supply of wine, the wine jug was as full as ever, even though it had been emptied several times. Clearly, their guests could not be the poor travelers they appeared to be. Such a miracle must be the magic of immortals. Immediately, the couple fell to their knees, begging the gods' forgiveness for the meager dinner they had served and the shabbiness of their tiny home.

Embarrassed at his poverty, Philemon got up quickly from his knees and ran outside, hoping to catch the couple's goose in order to cook it as a more appropriate dinner offering for the gods. But the goose sensed the old man's purpose and ran away. Finally, the goose ran straight into the house and jumped into Zeus's lap for protection. Zeus laughed, and told the old man to stop his chasing. The god assured the couple that he did not wish to eat their only goose.

Still smiling, Zeus and Hermes said, "Come with us, Baucis and Philemon. You have been wonderful hosts, and you shall be rewarded. However, the rest of the people in this country shall be punished for their rudeness."

Nervously, Baucis and Philemon followed as the gods hiked to the top of the hill behind their house. When they turned to look down at the valley, the couple was dismayed to see that all the houses in the village—except their own—had disappeared under the waters of a huge flood. Now, only the tips of the highest rooftops could be seen peeking out above the raging waters. The flood had swept in so quickly and so silently that the entire village had been surprised. Baucis and Philemon could not see a soul left in their town. All that was left was their own tiny home, the floodwaters lapping at its doorway.

On the high hill, safe and dry above the flood, Baucis and Philemon looked down again at their farm, unable to speak. Amazed, they watched as their house changed before their eyes into a magnificent temple made of gold and marble. They had no idea why this was happening. When they looked questioningly to the gods for an answer, Zeus smiled kindly and said, "You shall have your reward now. Tell me your wish, and you shall have it."

For a moment, Baucis and Philemon whispered together; they needed only a minute to decide what their wish would be. First, they asked the gods if they could be priests in the shiny gold temple that now stood in place of their house. Then they begged the gods to allow them to die both at the same moment, so that neither would ever have to live without the other.

Zeus granted the couple their first wish right away. Before returning with Hermes to Mount Olympus, Zeus sent Baucis and Philemon off to serve in the great temple that now stood where their farm used to be. The couple lived happily there for many years, growing very old but remaining ever faithful to the gods and to each other.

One day, while standing outside the temple, Baucis saw her husband's body stiffen. Right before her eyes, Philemon's feet grew into the ground, and leaves sprouted out of his hands. Baucis was shocked, but suddenly she realized that her own body was also sprouting roots and leaves. The couple had only a moment to say a loving goodbye before they both turned into trees, their trunks touching and their leaves mingling. In this way, the gods fulfilled their promise to Baucis and Philemon—they would never be apart, even in death.

After this startling event, the people who came to live again in Phrygia always told the couple's story and hung wreaths on the trees that grew twisted together outside the golden temple. In this way, the people of Phrygia honored the spirit of Baucis and Philemon, the kind and faithful couple who were rewarded by the gods for their kindness to others.

QUESTIONS AND ANSWERS

Q: *How was one supposed to treat a guest in ancient Greece?*

A: It was customary to treat guests or strangers with respect and hospitality. Even if a visitor was a complete stranger, he or she was expected to be treated with kindness.

Q: *Why did Zeus and Hermes visit Phrygia in disguise?*

A: The gods disguised themselves so they could see how the people treated ordinary guests and strangers.

Q: *What happened to the people who refused to invite the strangers into their homes?*

A: They disappeared under the waters of a huge flood.

Q: *Why did Zeus and Hermes punish the people of Phrygia?*

A: The people of Phrygia had been rude and inhospitable. This made the gods angry.

Q: *Why did the gods reward Baucis and Philemon?*

A: The couple was kind and followed the Greek custom of respecting strangers and travelers. Although they were poor and had little to eat, they shared whatever they had.

Q: *Why did Baucis and Philemon turn into trees?*

A: By becoming trees, Baucis and Philemon were able to remain together, even after their deaths. The touching trees are a symbol of their everlasting life together.

EXPERT COMMENTARY

The story of Baucis and Philemon includes a devastating flood, a symbolic event that appears in the creation stories of many cultures as well as in other Greek myths. Richmond Y. Hathorn explains the frequency of flood stories in mythology:

> Floods are a recurrent natural phenomenon, and flood-stories are a worldwide mythical phenomenon. To connect any particular flood-story with any particular flood is to confound myth, science, and history. . . .There are lesser flood-stories in Greek mythology; the best-known in other mythologies are, of course, Noah's in the Bible and Utnapishtim's in The Epic of Gilgamesh.[1]

Hathorn goes on to explain why floods are such a useful symbol. He writes:

> Floods suitably symbolize the end of one era and the beginning of another because they are baptisms *in extenso*: water destroys, kills, cleanses, purifies, revivifies, and is the stuff of new life.[2]

The importance of hospitality in ancient Greece was also an expectation well known to people of other cultures. Classicist Barry B. Powell explains:

> Above all, Zeus protected the custom called *xenia*, which we can roughly translate as "a formal institution of friendship." *Xenia* enabled Greeks to travel safely to distant lands where other Greeks lived. A relationship was established when a wanderer [*xenos* means "guest," or stranger] was received into someone's household, entertained, and given a gift. Should the host one day visit the wanderer's home, he could expect to be received similarly. Obligations of reciprocal hospitality fell not only on the individuals involved originally, but also on their entire families and on their descendants.[3]

8

ECHO AND
NARCISSUS

INTRODUCTION

Many myths rely on the metamorphosis, or transformation, of a character in order to explain the existence or appearance of certain animals, plants, strange land formations, or odd events that occur in the world.

Metamorphoses are a common theme in Greek myths. In many, the climax of a story is reached when a main character changes from a person into an entirely different creature. This type of change occurs through the intervention of a god. The story of Echo and Narcissus is one such story. Sometime around A.D. 8, the Roman poet Ovid wrote one version of this story in his work called *The Metamorphoses*, a fifteen-volume epic poem that relates more than two hundred stories. Ironically, the Roman work *The Metamorphoses* remains one of the most significant contributions to our knowledge of Greek mythology today.

The tale of Echo and Narcissus relates the story of the tragic love of a nymph for a young man. Nymphs were minor nature goddesses who were usually represented as beautiful maidens living in the mountains, forests, trees, or water. Echo was a talkative mountain nymph who fell in love with Narcissus, the son of the river-god Cephisus. Neither Echo nor Narcissus was worshipped as part of any religious ceremony in ancient Greece, but their story became important to explain otherwise unfathomable natural occurrences.

ECHO AND NARCISSUS

Echo was a beautiful mountain nymph who was a favorite friend of Artemis, the goddess of the hunt and a special protector of maidens. Echo, friendly and fun-loving, adored talking to her many sisters and friends. Nevertheless, no one ever complained that she talked too much, because Echo was so much fun to be with, and everyone loved her.

One of the other nymphs was having a love affair with Zeus, the king of the gods. Often, the couple would meet in a secret glade in the forest, far from the jealous eyes of Hera, Zeus's wife. Echo did not know about the affair, and she did not mind when her friends and sisters asked her to stand guard outside the secret glade. She never even thought to ask them why the glade needed guarding. All that Echo knew was that her sisters and friends warned her that her most important job was to keep Hera away from the glade.

Before long, Hera heard rumors that her husband was having an affair, and she became determined to find out which nymph was tempting her husband away. As she entered the forest and neared the glade, Hera saw Echo lounging near a shady group of trees. It was clear to Echo that Hera wanted to enter the glade, and, remembering her sisters' warning, Echo struck up a friendly conversation with the goddess, trying to distract her. While Echo was busy chatting with Hera, Zeus and his lover heard Hera's unmistakable voice and managed to escape before they could be discovered.

When Hera finally insisted on entering the glade and found that her husband had gotten away, she was furious! And even though Echo had played no part at all in Zeus's affair, Hera decided to punish her. In a high, shrill voice, the queen of the gods pronounced, "Young lady, your chattering has done you in, and you will be punished for it! From this moment forward, the only words you will ever be able to utter will be exactly those words, no more and no less, that other people have said to you first."

Echo was very upset. She had not meant to make Hera angry. She had only been helping her sisters and friends. Now she was burdened with an unbearable punishment, especially for someone who loved to talk! It seemed like nothing could be worse than silence or being doomed to repeat someone else's words.

Sadly, Echo left the glade, waving silently to her sisters and friends and wondering what she was going to do. Distracted by her thoughts, Echo suddenly found herself near a beautiful pond. There, sitting at the water's edge, was the handsomest young man Echo had ever seen. Desperately, Echo wished to make conversation with this youth, whose name was Narcissus, but since she had no way to talk to him, the young nymph hid herself behind a tree and watched to see what he was doing.

Narcissus was so good-looking that people were constantly falling in love with him at first sight. He was tall and naturally strong, and his curly hair was cut in such a way that it framed his elegant face. Having never seen himself, however, Narcissus had no idea how handsome he was, and he never understood why he received so much attention from those around him. In fact, that very day he had come into the forest trying to get away from all the people who had been gawking at him.

Thirsty from his long walk, Narcissus decided to stop at the pond for a drink. As he knelt before the still water, he saw the most beautiful face staring back at him from beneath the wet surface. But when he reached down to touch the beautiful person in the water, the face got blurry and quickly disappeared. Narcissus was so saddened at the disappearance of the beautiful water person that he sat back on the bank and cried. A few minutes later, he looked into the pond. There was the beautiful face, looking back at him. This time there were sad tears streaming down the handsome face. Narcissus felt sorry for the beautiful water person. He reached into the water to try to comfort him, but once again, the water person disappeared.

Suddenly, Narcissus heard a rustling in the leaves behind him. He did not know that Echo was hiding nearby, waiting for her chance to attract his attention. Startled and saddened by the disappearance of the beautiful person in the water, Narcissus called out, "Who's there?" In reply, Echo answered, "Who's there?" Since she could only repeat the youth's words, as Hera had commanded her, this was all the conversation she could manage. Echo thought Narcissus was beautiful indeed, and she was beginning to fall in love with him. Ashamed of her inability to speak, however, she remained hidden. Narcissus was surprised to hear his words flung back to him, and he was a little annoyed. Why would anyone be so rude as to repeat the words of someone else? Exasperated, Narcissus turned his attention to the person he saw in the water.

Each time Narcissus tried to touch the water, the beautiful person disappeared. Narcissus did not realize that there was no person living beneath the surface of the water and that he was actually seeing his own reflection. There was only Narcissus sitting on the bank, looking into the pond. As the sun set behind the trees, the youth could no longer see his reflection in the water. Calling out to the person he believed to live under the surface of the pond, Narcissus cried, "Wait! You are so beautiful! I love you!" All he heard in reply was the sound of Echo's voice repeating his words from her hiding place among the trees.

Narcissus had fallen deeply in love with the person he

thought he saw in the water, just as Echo had fallen in love
with him. Day after day, the youth and the nymph sat near
the pond, Narcissus staring at his reflection and Echo
staring at him. Narcissus pined for his appearing and
disappearing love, and Echo sat nearby, fists clenched in
frustration, wishing she could speak her own thoughts.

As time went by, the unhappy lovers forgot to sleep,
eat, or drink, so distracted were they by their unfulfilled
loves. After some time, Narcissus noticed that the person
in the water had grown thin and tired. He did not

understand that it was he who was withering away. From her hiding place, Echo could see Narcissus wasting away, but she could not see how equally gaunt she was becoming herself.

Day after day, Narcissus became more and more distraught as he sat by the bank of the pond, staring mournfully at the water. One day, overcome with frustration, he called out, "My love, why do you ignore me? Do you not see that I am dying for you?" Hiding in the woods, Echo responded, "My love, why do you ignore me? Do you not see that I am dying for you?" Consumed by his own overwhelming sadness, Narcissus took no notice of the nymph's repetitive answers. He leaned down, clutching at the water, but he could no longer go on. Exhausted, Narcissus died by the water's edge, trying to embrace his mysterious lover.

At the moment of his death, the gods took pity on the youth and his misdirected love and turned him into the flower called the narcissus. Echo, watching her love transform into a beautiful flower before her eyes, wept silently from her hiding place in the forest. Thus weeping, she died too, leaving only her echoing voice behind.

QUESTIONS AND ANSWERS

Q: *What type of goddess was Echo?*

A: She was a mountain nymph, a type of minor nature goddess.

Q: *Why did Hera punish Echo?*

A: Hera had come to the forest to find her husband, Zeus, with his lover. Because Echo chatted so much and distracted her, Hera was unable to catch him. She punished Echo for interfering with her plans.

Q: *What was Echo's punishment?*

A: She would no longer be able to speak her own mind. She would only be allowed to repeat what others had said first.

Q: *What happened when Narcissus looked in the pond?*

A: He saw his reflection in the water and thought there was a beautiful person living beneath the water. Narcissus fell so deeply in love with the person he saw in the water that he did not realize he was actually seeing a reflection of himself.

Q: *Why did Echo and Narcissus die?*

A: Echo and Narcissus both died of unrequited, or unfulfilled, love. They became so obsessed by their love that they stopped taking care of themselves and withered away.

Q: *What are some aspects of nature explained by the connected myths of Echo and Narcissus?*

A: The connected stories of Echo and Narcissus help explain the reflection of sound, known as echoing, and the nature of sight-reflection, such as images in water or mirrors. The introduction of the narcissus flower is also suggested here.

EXPERT COMMENTARY

At the end of this story, both characters change, or metamorphose, into different aspects of nature. Echo becomes the repetition of sound, and Narcissus becomes a flower. Before Ovid, the myths of Echo and Narcissus seem to have been considered separately. Richmond Y. Hathorn explains:

> Either Ovid . . . or some predecessor must have combined the stories of Echo and Narcissus because of the associated ideas of sound-reflection and sight-reflection.[1]

There is also a moral to this story. Narcissus's death and transformation demonstrate the danger of excessive self-love. The English language has borrowed Narcissus's name to decribe the term now commonly used for such self-obsessive love: *narcissism*. The story of Narcissus illustrates the dangers of this type of behavior:

> People with *narcissistic* personality disorder have a grandiose sense of self-importance. They seek excessive admiration from others and fantasize about unlimited success or power. They believe they are special, unique, or superior to others. However, they often have very fragile self-esteem.[2]

Echo's story is one that inspired much superstition in ancient Greece. Although she was not worshipped as a goddess, Echo was regarded as an important figure in Greek mythology. Hathorn describes her place in ancient Greek society:

> Echo had a shrine in Athens, but seems not really to have had a place in Greek cult. Her myth owes more to superstition than to religion; in folklore echoes are often thought to be answers given by supernatural voices.[3]

9

HELIUS AND PHAETHON

INTRODUCTION

Many Greek myths illustrate the trials and errors of human existence. Often characters are punished for failing to recognize their limitations. The Greek word *hubris* is often used to describe the human tendency to overstep one's boundaries. Sometimes people in myths exhibit hubris by challenging the authority of a ruler or a god. Hubris is sometimes thought to be the result of excessive pride. Unfortunately, acts of hubris usually end in tragedy. Hubris and the way it may be encouraged by peer pressure are touched on in the story of Helius and Phaethon.

Helius, the god of the sun (*helios* is the Greek word for sun), was the son of the Titan gods, Hyperion and Theia. Although he was an important figure because of his power over the sun, Helius was not worshipped in any significant way by the ancient Greeks. Often he was linked to, and sometimes confused with, Apollo, the god of light. Helius had many mistresses with whom he had many children. One of his lovers was Clymene, an oceanid, or spirit of the sea, the daughter of the Titan gods Oceanus and Tethys. Helius and Clymene had a son, Phaethon, whose name means "shining."

The story of Helius and Phaethon is told by Ovid in his *Metamorphoses*. It is another story that helps explain certain wonders of nature. In this story, we are offered explanations for the origins of the Milky Way galaxy and the deserts of Africa. The story also mentions real places— Ethiopia in Africa and the Eridanus River, which is often thought to be the modern Po River in Italy.[1]

HELIUS AND PHAETHON

Helius was the god of the sun. He ruled no particular area on the earth's surface because he had not been present when Zeus was busy assigning jobs to the gods. Helius's main job was to ride a chariot across the sky each day. This chariot was very important because, in fact, it was the sun itself. The sun gave light and warmth to the earth, and its travels across the heavens caused day and night. Helius was careful never to let anything jeopardize the daily rising and setting of the sun.

Although he was very busy, Helius had an affair with Clymene, a mortal woman. Clymene lived in the geographical area that is now known as Ethiopia. The couple had a son named Phaethon. Soon after the birth of Phaethon, the love affair ended, and Clymene married a prince who raised the boy as his own son. The prince and Clymene had other children after their marriage, and they all lived very happily for many years.

The happiness of the royal family was shattered, however, when Clymene confided to Phaethon that her husband, the prince, was not the boy's real father. Clymene told Phaethon that his father was Helius, the sun god. Phaethon was amazed at what his mother told him.

Phaethon was so obsessed with this shocking news that he bragged about his important father to the other boys at school. However, the other boys did not believe him, and although they were his friends, the boys teased Phaethon about his story. They just could not believe that their friend was the son of a god, suspecting instead that this story was just another one of Phaethon's fantasies. One of his friends challenged Phaethon and said, "If Helius is really your father, show us some proof. Then we will believe you."

Determined to show his friends that he was telling the truth, Phaethon went home and asked his mother to help him prove that Helius was really his father. Clymene had no physical evidence available to prove that the god was her son's father. However, she promised to show Phaethon the way to Helius's palace where he could ask the god himself for some proof.

With his mother's directions, Phaethon easily found the god's palace. He could hardly believe his eyes when he saw it for the first time. It was the most magnificent building the boy had ever seen. In fact, it was probably one of the most beautiful palaces ever built. Nervously, Phaethon approached the majestic dais where Helius was sitting. The boy could not help but gawk at the splendor of everything around him. Huge pillars of bronze and gold held up the ceiling of the throne room, making the chamber sparkle with light. Even the god's throne, carved out of solid emerald, was exquisite. There were lesser gods, who acted as Helius's servants, milling about the room, adding to the god's majesty. These various gods were called Day, Month, Year, the Centuries, the Hours, and the Seasons.

Phaethon looked so much like his beautiful mother with his striking physique and intense eyes that Helius recognized him as his son right away. The god told Phaethon that, indeed, he was his father, just as Clymene had said. When Phaethon explained that he wished to have proof to show his friends, Helius was surprised but understanding. He told Phaethon, "By the River Styx in Hades, I swear to give you whatever proof you ask for." Phaethon knew that the god was serious when he said this because no one, not even a god, could go back on a promise sworn by the River Styx.

Then, with the assurance of this promise, Phaethon turned to Helius and said, "Father, I believe that I am your son. But I would like to prove it to my friends who teased me and claimed that I am only pretending that you are my father. I know that you are very careful about driving your chariot across the sky each day, but if I am your son, you will allow me to drive the chariot tomorrow so that everyone may see me riding in your place. Then they will believe that I am your son. They will see that I can be as strong and as brave as a god. Remember your promise, and let me drive your chariot."

As soon as he heard his son's request, Helius wished that he had not made such a rash, unbreakable promise. The sun god never allowed anyone else to drive his chariot for the simple reason that it was extremely difficult to manage. The horses were so unruly that they would obey no one but Helius. Even Zeus, the king of the gods, could not drive Helius's chariot. Helius begged his son to reconsider his request and to ask for some other kind of proof. He tried to make Phaethon understand the danger and futility of trying to drive the chariot. Even if he were Zeus himself, Helius stressed, Phaethon could easily be killed by trying to ride across the sky.

Despite these warnings, Phaethon was determined to drive the sky chariot. He reminded the god of his oath upon the River Styx. Thus, Helius was forced to allow the boy his wish, and he told his servants, the Hours, to hitch up the horses to prepare for the boy's departure.

Phaethon was bursting with excitement. He could hardly keep from shouting for joy as he watched the Hours prepare the horses. While the servants held the horses steady, Phaethon climbed into the chariot, grinning at his father, who looked on with dismay. "Father," Phaethon said assuringly, "Do not worry. I will show you all what a good driver I am. You will be so proud!" With a final wave, the young prince dismissed the servants and tugged on the flaming gold reins to urge the magnificent horses onward into the sky.

For one brief moment, the earth was bathed in a calm morning light. Helius began to breathe an audible sigh of relief—perhaps Phaethon would be able to drive the horses after all. Unfortunately, this moment of calm was soon shattered.

Almost immediately after leaving his father's palace with the chariot, Phaethon lost control of the horses. He just could not keep them on their path. The horses left the road they usually traveled and began to race in different directions. The boy did not feel at all like the powerful son of Helius, the ruler of the day and night. Instead, he was terrified, and he clutched the side of the chariot to keep from falling out. Mournfully, Helius watched his son's wild ride from his shimmering throne, but he could do nothing to stop the disobedient horses.

First, the chariot took Phaethon into the night sky where he caused such damage that a huge burnt trail was left behind wherever the chariot happened to touch down. This scar became the Milky Way, and even now the etchings of Phaethon's chariot ride can be seen streaking across the sky. After leaving the night, the horses raced

back toward earth, dragging their frightened driver behind them. The horses swooped down over the area near the earth's equator, where the land caught fire when the chariot touched it. These burned areas became the deserts of Africa.

News of Phaethon's disastrous ride soon made its way to Mount Olympus. Gaia, the first mother of the gods, begged the other gods to help save the earth from destruction. As they watched, the gods began to realize that the entire world would soon be burned to a crisp if they did not step in soon and somehow manage to stop the racing chariot. Although he did not want to kill Helius's son, Zeus knew that this idea would be the only way to save the earth. So Zeus hurled a bolt of lightning at Phaethon. His aim was good, and Phaethon fell out of the chariot to his death in the Eridanus River. The wild horses and the splintered chariot also fell into the river.

Although they were sorry that the boy had died, most of the gods were relieved to see that the earth had been merely scorched and not completely destroyed. At his forge, Hephaestus the blacksmith made Helius a new chariot so that the world would continue to enjoy day and night. The new chariot—covered in jewels and intricate carvings—was even more beautiful than the first, in memory of the god's lost son.

Helius's daughters, the Heliades, were so upset about their brother's death, however, that they gathered along the Eridanus River to weep for him. They cried so many tears and for so many years that the gods took pity on them and turned them into poplar trees that grew along the banks of the river; their abundant tears were turned into amber, which dropped from the trees into the river.

QUESTIONS AND ANSWERS

Q: *Who were Phaethon's parents?*

A: Phaethon's father was Helius, the god of the sun. His mother was Clymene, a mortal woman who lived in a land that is now Ethiopia. Later Clymene married a prince who raised Phaethon as his own son.

Q: *Why did Phaethon want proof that Helius was his father?*

A: Phaethon's friends did not believe that he was the son of a god. Their disbelief caused Phaethon to prove to his friends, and the world, that he was the child of a famous and important god.

Q: *Why was Helius upset by Phaethon's request to drive the sun chariot?*

A: Helius knew how dangerous it would be for his son to drive the chariot. Helius realized that he alone could control the horses. He knew that Phaethon would surely be hurt if he attempted such a dangerous ride.

Q: *What astrological and geographical areas did Phaethon's disastrous chariot ride create?*

A: When the runaway chariot raced off into the sky, the Milky Way was marked out for eternity. When it touched the earth, the deserts of Africa were created.

Q: *What is hubris?*

A: *Hubris* is the Greek word to describe a kind of pride that comes over people when they try to be better than the gods in some way. Phaethon committed an act of hubris when he insisted that he could drive the sun chariot across the sky. Phaethon refused to recognize his limitations. As a result, his life ended tragically.

EXPERT COMMENTARY

Barry B. Powell suggests that Ovid's version of the story has some very strong moral lessons. Powell writes:

> It is a good example how, in the hands of the urbane Roman Ovid, descriptions of the world's early days become a prettified fantasy embodying the teasing morals, "Don't be too curious about your origins, and don't get too big for your breeches!"[2]

The figure of Helius is often associated with the island of Rhodes. In his encyclopedia of Greek mythology, Richard Stoneman writes:

> To make up for [being allotted no specific region on earth], Zeus allotted [Helius] the newly arisen island of Rhodes, of which he became the patron. The Colossus of Rhodes was a bronze statue of Helius. His portion is an appropriate one as Rhodes claims to receive more hours of sunshine per year than any other place in the Mediterranean.[3]

The Greeks, like people of many other cultures, often looked up into the sky at night and saw constellations, or pictures in the arrangements of stars. The Greek poets Homer and Hesiod both mention constellations in their works.[4] In his book, *Greek Mythology*, Richmond Y. Hathorn explains that the story of Phaethon's wild ride across the sky was sometimes used to remember the location of certain stars. He says:

> Eventually the whole drama was transported to the sky: Eridanus became a constellation; Phaethon became *Auriga*, "the Charioteer"; and his sisters became the *Hyades*, "the Rainy Ones."[5]

 GLOSSARY

ambrosia—A drink, ointment, or perfume used by the gods. Demeter used such an ointment to anoint Demophoon, the baby prince of Eleusis.

archaeology—The study of ancient civilizations.

bacchantes—Female followers of the god Dionysus. These women often behaved like wild animals and seemed to have superhuman strength.

chaos—The disordered order of the universe before the beginning of time. Eventually, Gaia, the first goddess of the new world, divided it into earth, sky, and sea. The Greek work could also mean a wide open space or a deep cavern.

Cyclopes—The giant children of Gaia and Uranus who each had only one eye in the middle of the forehead. They were skilled craftsmen and made weapons for the Olympians in their revolt against the Titans.

dais—A raised platform where a throne is often placed.

echo—The reflection of sound in nature. The word comes from the name of the nymph who was restricted to repeating what other people said to her.

Eleusinian Mysteries—Secret religious ceremonies in honor of the goddess Demeter. They were held in Eleusis, the town where Demeter was thought to have stayed while mourning the marriage of her daughter to Hades, the god of the Underworld.

glade—A shady part of the forest.

hubris—Excessive pride. People commit acts of excessive pride when they ignore their limitations and go beyond their bounds. Such actions often end in tragedy.

metamorphosis—A change or transformation. In Greek myth, there are many instances where a person is changed into something else. For example, Narcissus undergoes such a change when he is turned into a flower.

narcissism—Self-love.

nymph—A minor goddess or divinity of nature. The nymphs were usually represented as beautiful maidens who dwelled in the mountains, forests, trees, or water.

oceanid—A spirit of the sea.

Olympia—A town in the western part of the Peloponnesus that has major temples to the Olympian gods, the ruins of which one can still visit.

Olympians—The group of gods and goddesses, including Zeus, who were descended from the Titans.

omen—A natural sign or occurance that can be interpreted to predict the future.

oracle—A prophet who interprets signs and omens.

pantheon—A group of gods and goddesses.

polytheistic—Believing in more than one god or goddess.

River Styx—An important river in the Underworld. If a vow was made on the name of this river, it could never be broken, not even by a god.

sickle—A curved knife used to harvest crops. Cronos used one to kill his father, Uranus.

Tartarus—A deep cavern where many of the Titans were locked up after the war between the Titans and the Olympians.

Titans—The gods and goddesses who were children of Gaia and Uranus. Their leader was Cronus, the father of the Olympian gods.

trident—A three-pronged spear. The Cyclopes made one for Poseidon, the god of the oceans, during the war between the Titans and the Olympians.

CHAPTER NOTES

Preface

1. Liddell & Scott, *Greek-English Lexicon* (Oxford, England: Clarendon Press, 1948). All further definitions of Greek words will rely on Liddell & Scott.

2. Mark P. O. Morford and Robert J. Lenardon, *Classical Mythology*, 6th ed. (New York: Longman, 1999), p. 16.

3. Barry B. Powell, *Classical Myth*, 2nd ed. (Upper Saddle River, N. J.: Prentice Hall, 1998), pp. 25-27.

4. Anne S. Baumgartner, *A Comprehensive Dictionary of the Gods* (New York: Wing Books, 1995), p. 201.

Chapter 1. Creation

1. Hesiod, Theogony, lines 110–115, <http://www.perseus. tufts.edu/cgibin/ptext?doc=Perseus%3Atext%3A1999.01. 0130&query=card%3D%234&loc=63> (October 30, 2000).

2. Lucilla Burn, *Greek Myths* (Austin: University of Texas Press, 1990), p. 9.

3. Ken Dowden, *The Uses of Greek Mythology* (New York: Routledge, 1992), p. 135.

4. John Pinsent, *Greek Mythology* (New York: Paul Hamlyn, 1969), p. 22.

Chapter 2. The War Between the Titans and the Olympians

1. Spyros Photinos, *Olympia: Complete Guide*, trans. Tina McGeorge and Colin MacDonald (Athens, Greece: Olympic Publications, 1989), p. 5.

2. Ibid., p. 7.

3. Mark P. O. Morford and Robert J. Lenardon, *Classical Mythology*, 6th ed. (New York: Longman, 1999), p. 75.

4. Richmond Y. Hathorn, *Greek Mythology* (Beirut, Lebanon: American University of Beirut Press, 1977), p. 8.

5. John Pinsent, *Greek Mythology* (New York: Paul Hamlyn, 1969), p. 25.

6. Morford and Lenardon, p. 48.

Chapter 3. Prometheus and Earth's First Inhabitants

1. Barry B. Powell, *Classical Myth*, 2nd ed. (Upper Saddle River, N. J.: Prentice Hall, 1998), p. 46.

2. Ibid., p. 115.

3. Mark P. O. Morford and Robert J. Lenardon, *Classical Mythology*, 6th ed. (New York: Longman, 1999), p. 61.

Chapter 4. Pandora

1. Richmond Y. Hathorn, *Greek Mythology* (Beirut, Lebanon: American University of Beirut Press, 1977), p. 47.

2. Mark P. O. Morford and Robert J. Lenardon, *Classical Mythology*, 6th ed. (New York: Longman, 1999), p. 60.

3. Barry B. Powell, *Classical Myth*, 2nd ed. (Upper Saddle River, N. J.: Prentice Hall, 1998), p. 122.

Chapter 5. Demeter and Persephone

1. Barry B. Powell, *Classical Myth*, 2nd ed. (Upper Saddle River, N. J.: Prentice Hall, 1998), pp. 237-241.

2. Michael Grant, *Myths of Greeks and Romans* (New York: Meridian, 1995), p. 136.

3. Powell, p. 239.

4. Ibid., p. 237.

Chapter 6. Dionysus and his Followers

1. Richmond Y. Hathorn, *Greek Mythology* (Beirut, Lebanon: American University of Beirut Press, 1977), p. 282.

2. Ibid., p. 135.

3. *Mythology, An Illustrated Guide*, Roy Willis, ed. (New York: Barnes and Noble, Inc., 1998), p. 141.

4. Barry B. Powell, *Classical Myth*, 2nd ed. (Upper Saddle River, N. J.: Prentice Hall, 1998), p. 267.

Chapter 7. Baucis and Philemon

1. Richmond Y. Hathorn, *Greek Mythology* (Beirut, Lebanon: American University of Beirut Press, 1977), p. 18.

2. Ibid.

3. Barry B. Powell, *Classical Myth* 2nd ed. (Upper Saddle River, N. J.: Prentice Hall, 1998), pp. 140-141.

Chapter 8. Echo and Narcissus

1. Richmond Y. Hathorn, *Greek Mythology* (Beirut, Lebanon: American University of Beirut Press, 1977), p. 106.

2. "Personality Disorders," *Microsoft® Encarta® Encyclopedia 99.* © 1993–1998 Microsoft Corporation.

3. Hathorn, p. 106.

Chapter 9. Helius and Phaethon

1. Barry B. Powell, *Classical Myth* 2nd ed. (Upper Saddle River, N. J.: Prentice Hall, 1998), p. 81.

2. Ibid.

3. Richard Stoneman, *Greek Mythology: An Encyclopedia of Myth and Legend.* (London: Diamond Books, 1995), p. 84.

4. "Constellation (astronomy)," *Microsoft® Encarta® Encyclopedia 99.* © 1993–1998 Microsoft Corporation.

5. Richmond Y. Hathorn, *Greek Mythology* (Beirut, Lebanon: American University of Beirut Press, 1977), p. 51.

📖 FURTHER READING 📖

Barber, Antonia. *Apollo & Daphne: Masterpieces of Greek Mythology*. New York: Oxford University Press, 1998.

D'Aulaire, Ingri and Edgar Parin D'Aulaire. *D'Aulaire's Book of Greek Myths*. New York: Bantam Doubleday Dell, 1992.

Fleischman, Paul. *Dateline Troy*. Cambridge, Mass.: Candlewick Press, 1996.

Graves, Robert. *Greek Gods and Heroes*. New York: Bantam Doubleday Dell, 1995.

Hamilton, Virginia. *In the Beginning: Creation Stories from Around the World*. New York: Harcourt Brace Jovanovich, 1988.

Lies, Betty Bonham. *Earth's Daughters: Stories of Women in Classical Mythology*. Golden, Col.: Fulcrum Publishing, 1999.

Loewen, Nancy. *Zeus*. Mankato, Minn.: Capstone Press, 1999.

———. *Athena*. New York: RiverFront Books, 1999.

———. *Hercules*. New York: RiverFront Books, 1999.

McCaughrean, Geraldine. *Greek Gods and Goddesses*. New York: Simon & Schuster, 1998.

Stephanides, Menalaos. *The Gods of Olympus*. Athens, Greece: Sigma, 1999.

Vinge, Joan D. *The Random House Book of Greek Myths*. New York: Random House, 1999.

Yeoh Hong Nam. *Greece*. Milwaukee, Wis.: Gareth Stevens, Inc., 1999.

INTERNET ADDRESSES

The Ancient City of Athens

<http://www.indiana.edu/~kglowack/athens/>

A photo tour of archeological sites in Athens.

The Encyclopedia Mythica

<http://www.pantheon.org/mythica/>

Explores articles about various Greek gods. Also covers other types of mythology.

Greek Mythology

<http://www.greekmythology.com/index.html>

A list of gods, myths, and places. Brief descriptions with links throughout.

Greek Mythology: A Look Back in Time

<http://library.thinkquest.org/18650/>

A ThinkQuest site written by students for students. Includes information about constellations.

Greek Mythology: From the Iliad to the Last Tyrant

<http://www.messagenet.com/myths>

Information, links to other interesting sites, and a fun quiz game for all ages.

Greek Mythology Link

<http://hsa.brown.edu/~maicar/>

Some pages also available in Spanish. For the advanced reader.

The Illustrated Encyclopedia of Greek Mythology

<http://www.cultures.com/greek_resources/greek_
encyclopedia/greek_encyclopedia_home.html>

Mythweb

<http://www.mythweb.com/>

Illustrations, interesting facts and stories, and information for teachers.

The Perseus Project

<http://www.perseus.tufts.edu/>

Information about classical texts and their translations, archaeology, and more.

⊡ INDEX ⊡